M000033717

How to Succeed in College and Beyond

Also by Daniel R. Schwarz

Reading the European Novel to 1900 (2014)

Endtimes: Crises and Turmoil at the New York Times (2012; new revised paperback edition 2014)

In Defense of Reading: Teaching Literature in the Twenty-First Century (2008)

Reading the Modern British and Irish Novel 1890–1930 (2005)

Broadway Boogie Woogie: Damon Runyon and the Making of New York City Culture (2003)

Rereading Conrad (2001)

Imagining the Holocaust (1999; revised edition 2000)

Reconfiguring Modernism: Explorations in the Relationship between Modern Art and Modern Literature (1997)

Narrative and Representation in the Poetry of Wallace Stevens: "A Tune Beyond Us, Yet Ourselves" (1993)

The Case for a Humanistic Poetics (1991)

The Transformation of the English Novel, 1890–1930: Studies in Hardy, Conrad, Joyce, Lawrence, Forster, and Woolf (1989; revised edition 1995)

Reading Joyce's "Ulysses" (1987; centenary edition 2004)

The Humanistic Heritage: Critical Theories of the English Novel from James to Hillis Miller (1986; revised edition 1989)

Conrad: The Later Fiction (1982)

Conrad: "Almayer's Folly" to "Under Western Eyes" (1980)

Disraeli's Fiction (1979)

As Editor

Damon Runyon: Guys and Dolls and Other Writings (2008)

The Early Novels of Benjamin Disraeli, 6 volumes (consulting editor, 2004)

Conrad's "The Secret Sharer" (Bedford Case Studies in Contemporary Criticism, 1997)

Joyce's "The Dead" (Bedford Case Studies in Contemporary Criticism, 1994)

Narrative and Culture (with Janice Carlisle, 1994)

How to Succeed in College and Beyond

and Beyond

The Art of Learning

Daniel R. Schwarz

WILEY Blackwell

This edition first published 2016
© 2016 John Wiley & Sons, Ltd.

Registered Office
John Wiley & Sons, Ltd, The Atrium, Southern Gate, Chichester, West Sussex, PO19 8SQ, UK

Editorial Offices
350 Main Street, Malden, MA 02148-5020, USA
9600 Garsington Road, Oxford, OX4 2DQ, UK
The Atrium, Southern Gate, Chichester, West Sussex, PO19 8SQ, UK

For details of our global editorial offices, for customer services, and for information about how
to apply for permission to reuse the copyright material in this book please see our website
at www.wiley.com/wiley-blackwell.

The right of Daniel R. Schwarz to be identified as the author of this work has been asserted in
accordance with the UK Copyright, Designs and Patents Act 1988.

All rights reserved. No part of this publication may be reproduced, stored in a retrieval system, or
transmitted, in any form or by any means, electronic, mechanical, photocopying, recording or
otherwise, except as permitted by the UK Copyright, Designs and Patents Act 1988, without the prior
permission of the publisher.

Wiley also publishes its books in a variety of electronic formats. Some content that appears in print
may not be available in electronic books.

Designations used by companies to distinguish their products are often claimed as trademarks. All
brand names and product names used in this book are trade names, service marks, trademarks or
registered trademarks of their respective owners. The publisher is not associated with any product or
vendor mentioned in this book.

Limit of Liability/Disclaimer of Warranty: While the publisher and author have used their best efforts
in preparing this book, they make no representations or warranties with respect to the accuracy or
completeness of the contents of this book and specifically disclaim any implied warranties of
merchantability or fitness for a particular purpose. It is sold on the understanding that the publisher is
not engaged in rendering professional services and neither the publisher nor the author shall be liable
for damages arising herefrom. If professional advice or other expert assistance is required, the services
of a competent professional should be sought.

Library of Congress Cataloging-in-Publication data applied for

Hardback 9781118974841
Paperback 9781118974858

A catalogue record for this book is available from the British Library.

Set in 10.5/12.5pt Bembo by SPi Global, Pondicherry, India
Printed and bound in Malaysia by Vivar Printing Sdn Bhd

1   2016

For my past and present students; my wife, Marcia Jacobson;
and my sons, David and Jeffrey Schwarz

Contents

Contents

Part IV   The Value of the Humanities   109

Part V   Perspectives of a Professor   141

Acknowledgments

I have been especially fortunate in teaching at Cornell for 47 years. I want to express my gratitude and appreciation to my current and recent students as well as to the generations of students I have taught, especially the many I have kept in touch with over the years.

I cannot mention all those students and colleagues – here and elsewhere – whom I quote and the many others with whom I have discussed aspects of my book and from whom I have learned, but I want to extend my heartfelt thanks.

Three visiting professorships and short visits to many campuses in the US and abroad as well as my directing nine National Endowment for the Humanities (NEH) Summer Seminars for college teachers and high school teachers have enabled me to widen my experience.

I am most grateful for the splendid work that Pauline Shongov, a Cornell Presidential Research Scholar, contributed to the manuscript. Helen Maxson has been a terrific reader of the close-to-final draft. The suggestions of Mark Eisner, Harvard '60 and Cornell Ph.D. '70, Senior Lecturer in the Cornell School of Operations Research and Engineering 1997–2007, have been extremely helpful at both the microcosmic and macrocosmic level. I continually learn from my conversations with my friend and colleague Laura Brown. David Duchamp keeps me informed about the STEM (science, technology, engineering, and mathematics) world and Ron Ehrenburg is a great resource on the economics of the university. I also need to acknowledge the late Phillip Marcus and the late M.H. Abrams for insights over the years.

I am grateful to the English Department faculty and staff, and especially to Vicky Brevetti, for creating a supportive and pleasurable work environment.

Acknowledgments

Earlier versions of some chapters have been published in the *Huffington Post* (http://www.huffingtonpost.com/daniel-r-schwarz/) and an early version of chapter 19 appeared in the *Cornell Alumni Magazine*.

It is hard to overstate my debt to my wife, Marcia Jacobson, my best friend and the most perceptive reader and editor I know. Her input is on every page.

Daniel R. Schwarz
Cornell University
Ithaca, New York
October, 2015

1

Introduction: How to Succeed in College and Beyond: The Art of Learning

Purpose: Preparing Students for College

The purpose of this book is to help prepare students, parents, and high school advisors for the college experience and beyond. My goal is to help students balance the joy of learning with the practicality of finding a career path. This book is for all those contemplating a college education and for their families, as well as for those already admitted to college.

Important questions are being asked today about American higher education. Not only are the value of a college education and the economics of colleges and universities under scrutiny, but so too is the concept of the American dream whereby people use their ability and education to fulfill their potentials and move up the socio-economic ladder. On the one hand, colleges and universities do have more diverse student bodies than in the past. But on the other, evidence of severe economic inequality and social injustice dominates the news. Inequality and injustice are causes and effects of a crisis in America that extends to the role of higher education. I address those issues in the context of offering ideas for applying to and succeeding in college, including how to apply for financial aid and how to limit burdensome loans that hamper the future.

I suggest initiatives that might help middle- and working-class parents and their children who cannot afford to send their children to expensive private schools or to live in affluent communities with elite public schools. In these affluent communities, preparation for college dominates virtually every educational policy decision made by school administrators and Boards of Education. In such school districts, parents are in the foreground encouraging

How to Succeed in College and Beyond: The Art of Learning, First Edition. Daniel R. Schwarz.
© 2016 John Wiley & Sons, Ltd. Published 2016 by John Wiley & Sons, Ltd.

their children, playing roles in shaping school policy, and contributing to foundations that supplement the tax base for the purposes of supporting extra-curricular activities, including athletics. These parents also pay for their children's private tutors and sports coaches. By contrast, in many rural and urban schools, graduation rates are low, school budgets are pinched, teachers are overworked and deal with serious discipline issues on a daily basis, guidance counselors are asked to serve far too many students, and parents struggling to make a living do not have time or funds to be advocates for their children.

In early fall 2014, in an op-ed piece for the *US News* as he began his ninth and last year as the President of Cornell, David Skorton asked vital questions:

> For the first time in my 36 years in academia, the value of America's colleges and universities is being questioned – and seriously. Is what we offer worth the money and time invested? Will a college degree really translate into a better job down the road or improve our quality of life? Couldn't we rely more on technology and less on highly paid faculty members and expensive campuses and student amenities to deliver our "product" at lower cost?

In part, this book is a response to issues raised by these questions.

While my primary focus is on the US system of higher education, my suggestions are transferable to the educational systems of other countries. Young adults seeking higher education everywhere face similar challenges and pressures, although the US is unique in the financial issues students face. While career opportunities vary from country to country, balancing the joy of learning with the necessity and reality of career preparation is a pervasive issue.

I draw upon my 47 years as a Professor of English, but also the experience of colleagues and students at other universities in the US and other countries. My appointment has been at Cornell, but I have held visiting professorships at the main campus of the University of Hawaii, the University of Alabama at Huntsville (which is one of the Alabama state system's four research universities along with Tuscaloosa, Auburn, and Birmingham), and at the University of Arkansas (Little Rock). As Director of five NEH (National Endowment for the Humanities) Summer Seminars for College Teachers, I have also worked with faculty from a wide variety of colleges. I have also directed four NEH Summer Programs for school teachers in which virtually all my participants were secondary school English teachers working with Advanced Placement classes and were knowledgeable about college preparation.

I have consulted hundreds of students and scores of colleagues for input on this book. This book is about the college experience and how to make the most of it, including not only the available resources for financial aid, but also ways for students to prepare for their economic futures.

Much has been written of late about the shortcomings of American colleges and universities, with a focus on the relatively little time students spend on their academic study, the excessive partying that turns campuses into permissive social circuses and sites of sexual abuse, and the burgeoning costs accompanied by excessive student loans. I will take up these legitimate concerns in the pages that follow. Although prior research about the economics of the university is not my primary focus, I will on occasion address how and why research universities balance their priorities in light of limited resources. While both acknowledging the shortcomings of American colleges and universities and praising their strengths, I will propose ways for students to get the most out of their higher education.

This finding fault with American higher education includes not only William Deresiewicz's *Excellent Sheep: The Miseducation of the American Elite and the Way to a Meaningful Life* and the CNN documentary *Ivory Tower* but also Kevin Carey's *The End of College: Creating the Future of Learning and the University of Everywhere*, and, to a lesser extent, Frank Bruni's *Where You Go Is Not Who You'll Be: An Antidote to the College Admissions Mania.*

Yes, I do believe that the most highly endowed universities and colleges could do better at controlling their rising tuition by drawing more on their endowments – that is, by increasing the payout rate of their endowments. Colleges and universities could also ask their most generous donors to contribute more to their year-to-year expenses rather than to endowments. In the case of the wealthiest schools like Harvard, Yale, Princeton, and Stanford, their endowments are so large that a case could be made for their not charging tuition to any students.

Owing to the rising prices of stocks and bonds, and taking into consideration major fluctuations in those assets, the ratio of payouts to total endowments has shrunk in the past two decades (see Ehrenberg, *Tuition Rising*, 35–49). At Cornell, a mere half percent increase in the payout would result in approximately $31 million, based on a $6.2 billion endowment. Indeed, to meet the competitive need to raise financial aid to at least approach its much wealthier peers, the payout was raised from 2010–11 to 2014–15, but there is no way that Cornell can keep up with the much larger endowments of Harvard, Yale, Princeton, and Stanford.

A significant issue is how to open the doors of higher education, including those of the most prestigious schools, to those in the lower economic and social strata. In a report by Barry Bergman for the *Berkeley News*, Goldie Blumenstyk, author of *American Higher Education in Crisis? What Everyone Needs to Know*, asserts:

> [Y]ou'll still find lower-income students and minority students far more concentrated in community colleges and for-profit colleges, and upper-income students and white students more concentrated at four-year private colleges and publics. ...

3

[A]n adult from a wealthy family is nine times as likely to earn a bachelor's degree by the age of 24 as one from a poor family – with all the implications for social and financial success that entails.

A narrative of higher education in America should highlight the role of public education, including that of the great state universities like California and Michigan and the role that CUNY (City University of New York) played and still plays for first-generation Americans. When admission was exceedingly competitive, CCNY (City College of New York) produced a significant number of Nobel Prize winners, and one could argue that the University of California at Berkeley has been the pre-eminent university of the country if not the world. Unfortunately, the days of free and almost free tuition have passed. Nonetheless, the public universities still offer a lower-cost alternative to elite schools, particularly for residents of the state or city in which they are located.

The Economic Value of Higher Education

While I will be realistic about problems, I will be telling another, more optimistic story than many critics of American Higher Education. As Barry Glassner and Morton Schapiro wrote in the October 6, 2014 *Chronicle of Higher Education*:

> The vast majority of students graduate with relatively modest loans – under $30,000, on average – and almost one-third leave college with no debt at all. Meanwhile the college premium – the ratio of earnings by college graduates to those by high-school graduates – is at or near a record level.

MIT economist David Autor writes: "The economic payoff to college education rose steadily throughout the 1980s and 1990s and was barely affected by the Great Recession starting in 2007." According to Autor, that is true for a great many "developed countries." In the US, Autor finds that between 1965 and 2008 the value in lifetime earning of a university education, compared to those with a high school diploma, has "roughly tripled."

We are often told that college isn't for everyone, but it is surprising how many people can benefit from graduating from a four-year college. According to David Leonardt in an April 24, 2015 *New York Times* article entitled "College for the Masses":

> The unemployment rate among college graduates ages 25 to 34 is just 2 percent, even with the many stories you hear about out-of-work college graduates. They're not generally working in menial jobs, either. The pay gap between college graduates and everyone else is near a record high.

What needs to be stressed is that even students with less than sterling credentials benefit greatly from college, although among this group there is, as Leonardt further notes, a high drop-out rate:

> Less selective colleges often set [low] benchmarks: Students who score 840 on the SAT, for example, or maintain a C+ average in high school are admitted. Those who don't clear the bar are generally rejected, and many don't attend any four-year college. ... Perhaps most important, the data show that the students just above the admissions cutoff earned substantially more by their late 20s than students just below it – 22 percent more on average.

From the practical standpoint, we know the economic value of a college degree. In a 2014 *Chronicle of Higher Education* article entitled "Is a Degree Still Worth It? Yes, Researchers Say, and the Payoff Is Getting Better," Lance Lambert reports on a study by two researchers with the Federal Reserve of New York:

> Jaison R. Abel and Richard Deitz, found that ... a bachelor's degree for a 2013 graduate was worth $272,693, on average, and when adjusted for inflation, the value of a degree has hovered around $300,000 for more than a decade. ... Even though the wages for college graduates are not increasing, the gap between their pay and earnings of those with only a high-school diploma has increased, keeping the value of a college degree from falling.

Citing the same study in a *Wall Street Journal* piece entitled "A College Degree Pays Off Far Faster Than It Used To," Josh Mitchell writes:

> College graduates may be taking on historically high debt burdens to finance their educations. But it will take them far less time to get a return on that "investment" than it took their parents' generation. That's the conclusion of new research from the Federal Reserve Bank of New York. Researchers there estimate someone earning a bachelor's degree in 2013 will need 10 years to recoup the entire cost of that degree. Those who earned a bachelor's in 1983 needed 23 years to do so.

Thus we have incontrovertible evidence for the economic value of a four-year college degree.

College Education and Quality of Life

What about the value of a college education in non-economic and at times intangible terms? In a *New York Times* column entitled "Demanding More from College," Frank Bruni rightly complains "about the narrowness of the discussion [about the value of a college education], which so heavily emphasizes how a career is successfully forged and how financial security is quickly achieved."

In the pages that follow, I want to stress what education can add to students' quality of life in terms of self-awareness, understanding of the past and present contexts that define our individual experiences, and appreciation of the arts as a doorway to a fuller life. To those lifetime gifts, I need to add that education teaches us to solve problems, to read insightfully, to write lucidly and logically, to speak articulately, to think rigorously, and to be creative.

College can also make us more tolerant citizens by teaching us to be receptive to diverse ideas. In the same piece, Bruni observes:

> [T]here's another dimension to college, and it's one in which students aren't being served, or serving themselves, especially well. I'm referring to the potential – and need – for college to confront and change political and social aspects of American life that are as troubling as the economy. … [W]e should talk as much about the way college can establish patterns of reading, thinking and interacting that buck the current tendency among Americans to tuck themselves into enclaves of confederates with the same politics, the same cultural tastes, the same incomes. That tendency fuels the little and big misunderstandings that are driving us apart. It's at the very root of our sclerotic, dysfunctional political process.

Openness to rethinking past assumptions is a goal that fulfills both the joy and practicality of learning, for if students learn to communicate ideas in nuanced discourse, logically and lucidly presented in such a way that there is space for substantive discussion, we will have the pleasure of living in a less polarized and more civil society where democracy functions and diverse perspectives are respected. At best, college teaches democracy by teaching students not only to work cooperatively in classes and extra-curricular activities, but also to speak their minds, often with the hope of changing the minds of others.

Notwithstanding the shortcomings of US universities, they offer hope and possibility. While some of our American students may take this for granted, most of my students are aware that they are in a crucible of opportunity. Foreign students who come here understand that the United States and its better colleges offer them something special. In the words of Emma Ianni, Cornell '17, an undergraduate from Italy,

> I came here to find something that cannot be found [at home]: a bright future. My generation was born in a time that many define as the worst period for the job market since the Great Depression. Crisis, fear, and disillusionment are pandemic, but here at Cornell I did find something I could have never found in Italy, my home country: here in the United States I found that determined hope that everyone needs nowadays. I say "determined" because I don't mean hope in a sort of fatalistic way; it's not about lightheartedly waiting for things to work out;

it is rather about making things work out. ... But here, people from very early on learn that if they do extra-curriculars, if they fully commit to what they do, if they work hard enough, if they practice every day and don't give up when it gets hard, if they accept challenges and run for leadership positions in their clubs, then they will make it. And this is powerful.

Writing during the fall 2014 political crisis in Hong Kong, Gabriella Lee, Cornell '16, explains why Hong Kong students like herself appreciate the security of Cornell:

> With so much instability at home, it's easy to see why so many Hong Kong families find they need the security they feel an Ivy League education guarantees. ... I worry if I'll even be able to go home or if I will want to go home to a place that may eventually lack press freedom and government accountability, or a place where the police are ordered to openly tear gas peaceful protestors, or a place where local heritage and culture are wiped out in favor of big business interests.

Sally Ruge Gao, Cornell '15, who was an undergraduate from China, observes:

> I personally came to Cornell because I knew it offered me choice in learning whatever I wanted to learn, be it liberal arts or applied economics. ... An excellent education – in my opinion – teaches you to think critically and to have a good set of rational judgment abilities. ... Cornell and the Ivies give you choice in what you want to be educated in. ...The universities precisely teach you to not be a sheep, if you know how to listen. There will always be people who pawn Ivy degrees for high starting salaries.

Responding to Naysayers: College as Hope and Opportunity

In his *Excellent Sheep: The Miseducation of the American Elite and the Way to a Meaningful Life*, William Deresiewicz has complained about the shortcomings of education at what he calls elite schools – a list of which he never provides and a category he does not define precisely – and about how these schools encourage careerism and stifle creativity and boldness: "We want kids with resilience, self-reliance, independence of spirit, genuine curiosity and creativity; and a willingness to take risks and make mistakes" (236). In contrast, he praises some non-elite liberal arts colleges as places where teaching, rather than research, is valued and where the humanities are emphasized.

I am sure that this emphasis on teaching takes place at the world's prestigious public and private universities too, as well as throughout the American higher education system. Every day I see those qualities that Deresiewicz regrets missing. My Cornell classes and those of many of my colleagues are devoted to building those qualities even while we teach subjects. Moreover, I am speaking in this book not only about the elite schools, but also about the full range of American colleges.

Deresiewicz does have some interesting things to say about the ideals of a liberal education. I do agree with his objections to giving preference to legacies – the children of former graduates – in the admission process. Perhaps there are a small fraction of students who are busy building a CV as opposed to enjoying and immersing themselves in their studies. However, Deresiewicz's macrocosmic generalizations lack evidence, and his indictment of the "meritocracy" is reductive.

Certainly, in some urban and suburban places there is an anxiety epidemic on the part of parents worried that their children will not excel. I have heard parents in NYC worrying about getting their children into the best private nursery schools and even hiring people to prepare their three-year-old children for interviews. I have had students who had so much parental help and expensive private tutoring that, despite having terrific grades in private day schools and competitive public schools, they had trouble as first-term freshmen doing their own work.

But we need to understand that this anxiety epidemic is only one strand of the story of students making their way through the American educational system. I also see middle- and lower-income children – often first-generation college students – from less competitive public schools excelling at Cornell. Within a term they usually catch up with students from Horace Mann, Dalton, and Exeter as well as from elite public schools such as Stuyvesant, the Bronx High School of Science, and Boston Latin. Certainly upward mobility is alive and well, although, to be sure, were admission based purely on merit, the Ivies would take fewer legacies and potential varsity athletes. The latter, especially in so-called major sports like football, basketball, and hockey (as well as, at Cornell, wrestling), are heavily recruited by the coaches even though the Ivies don't give athletic scholarships.

Perhaps we professors and administrators need to do a better job responding to naysayers such as Deresiewicz. As Nicholas B. Dirks, Chancellor of the University of California at Berkeley, asserted in the July 22, 2014 *Chronicle of Higher Education*, "For too long we have neglected the need to aggressively defend, explain, and promote the value of the education our institutions provide, not just for individuals but for society as a whole." One goal of my book is to do just that while not overlooking areas that need improvement.

One of Deresiewicz's basic premises is that students have changed for the worse. He asserts that students were once more creative, imaginative, and interested in learning for its sake than they are now. My experience contradicts this claim.

We are also told that previous generations of students were happier, more confident, and had more developed "souls," a term Deresiewicz uses in a secular sense. Put another way, they were less anxious, stressed, and depressed, and more reflective about who they were. Of course, those who make these assertions do not provide substantive evidence or consider that prior generations were less likely to admit to depression and anxiety, because in the past admitting stress and depression or seeking help was culturally less acceptable.

Judged by the attention he received, Deresiewicz briefly touched a popular chord and became a rallying point for naysayers. Anxious parents whose children were not, or might not be, admitted to elite colleges could feel that little had been lost. While a great many of Deresiewicz's examples refer to Yale and Harvard and very few to Cornell, I believe much of what he says either is hyperbolic or lacks factual underpinnings: "Everybody [at elite colleges] thinks that they're the only one who's suffering, so nobody says anything, so everybody suffers. Everyone feels like a fraud, everyone thinks that everyone else is smarter than they are" (Deresiewicz, 16). Suffering is living under the fear of having one's home bombed, or being displaced from an area where one has lived for generations, or having a dread disease, or losing a beloved friend or family member. Suffering is not, in most cases, being concerned about your future when you are 19 years old and are attending an elite university in the United States. What Deresiewicz is describing is the discomfort that we all experience as young adults and, indeed, periodically thereafter.

Students from our current diverse ethnic and socio-economic backgrounds may have more anxiety than those admitted to elite schools two generations ago, but they succeed. Moreover, today colleges and universities admit students with emotional and physical challenges who might not have been able to function at college a few decades ago. We have far more support for deaf, blind, and other physically challenged students as well as those diagnosed with bi-polar disorders, depression, and dyslexia.

Did universities, especially elite ones, have higher standards in the past? If we use grades as our criterion, there is some reason to answer "Yes." Without doubt we have grade inflation, and one could argue that giving an A- for what 30 years ago was a B or B- is a lowering of standards. On the whole, however, I do not see a decline in the quality of academic work. I would argue that the quality of my students in terms of their preparation and performance is better than it once was. Moreover, while some students (being human) may occasionally take advantage of a professor's good will and trust, at Cornell I don't see much evidence of Deresiewicz's particular complaints: "[T]here are due dates and attendance requirements at elite colleges, but no one takes them seriously. Extensions are available for the asking; threats to deduct credit for missed classes are rarely, if ever, carried out. Kids at prestigious schools receive an endless string of second chances" (218). Is there anything wrong with a day or two extension for a student who is ill or temporarily overwhelmed?

Another area where standards may have suffered nationally is the amount of time students spend on their academic work, and I will discuss that issue in the pages that follow. Some of the time once spent on academic study has been replaced by the surge in the time spent on extra-curricular activities and employment. At non-elite schools, students often have jobs to pay for college and family needs, and these jobs may require that they work many hours a week and perhaps full-time. Furthermore, statistics show that a good deal of students' time is spent on social media. It is possible that more time than in the past is spent on what is now called "partying." Of course, how students use their time varies from student to student.

When I hear of my students' impressive range of extra-curricular activities, I realize how much more time I had in college for reading and thinking. Whatever strengths I have today as a teacher-scholar would be less developed had I not given priority to my studies as an undergraduate; those years built a base for my future work. I write now not to turn back the clock for today's students or to scold them for trying to do too much, but to share my own joy in learning.

The Joy and Practicality of Learning: Succeeding in College and Beyond

I begin with a chapter on how to prepare for college while in secondary school and even before that. I devote the next chapter to the complex process of choosing a college as well as the college application process and suggestions for getting financial aid. I then address in separate chapters each year of the four-year experience; in those chapters, I discuss such specific issues as time management, how to find mentors, whether to go abroad or take a term in Washington, DC, and planning for the future after graduation.

I include chapters on how to select classes as well as what parents need to know about the college experience. I discuss the pros and cons of the Greek system, that is, sororities and fraternities, and why I think, despite their importance to some students, that the Greek system may have outlived its usefulness.

Believing everyone should take some courses in the arts and the humanities (as well as gain a grounding in basic science and computer skills), I then turn to issues that pertain to the study of the arts and the humanities. What follows are chapters devoted to why we should study the arts, what we learn from them, and what kinds of employment and career possibilities are available to those with a BA in English and, by implication, in other fields in the arts and the humanities. I am responding to the widespread view that the study of the humanities is a passport to unemployment, if not to poverty. I also discuss the possibilities and advisability of getting a doctorate in the humanities.

I conclude with a section on my perspective as a professor. Because I think students and parents will benefit from knowing what a professor is thinking about when he or she organizes his/her courses, I discuss my goals and my philosophy as a teacher. I discuss the balance between teaching and research and why, despite some claims to the contrary, these two activities usually supplement one another. Finally, I discuss the values of the current generation of students and the current emphasis on community involvement. In doing so, I respond to the charge that contemporary students are self-immersed and less interested in the world than their predecessors.

Part I
Beginnings

2

How to Prepare for College

Introduction

Because I have been teaching at Cornell for more than four decades, and because I have been writing on higher education for the *Huffington Post* and in 2008 published *In Defense of Reading: Teaching Literature in the Twenty-First Century*, I am often asked if I have suggestions for preparing young people for college. The following suggestions are by no means exhaustive but provide some basics.

A student needs to develop the necessary skills to pursue a college degree, although in truth there are many kinds of colleges, and some are far more difficult than others in terms of both admittance and performance expectations. Not everyone is thinking about attending an elite college. For many, the right choice is the local branch of a state college, a community college for the first two years, or a small liberal arts college, none of which have the rigorous entry requirements of the Ivies, MIT, Caltech, Chicago, Stanford, Duke, Northwestern, the flagship campuses of major state universities (Michigan, Wisconsin, Indiana, UCLA, Berkeley, etc.), or the elite small liberal arts colleges (Amherst, Williams, Middlebury, Emory, the Claremont schools, etc.).

Before choosing a college, students need to consider why they want to go to college and what they expect to get out of the experience. Each student needs to assess what programs have value for him or her, not only in economic terms, but also in expanding his or her horizons and preparing for the fullest

How to Succeed in College and Beyond: The Art of Learning, First Edition. Daniel R. Schwarz.
© 2016 John Wiley & Sons, Ltd. Published 2016 by John Wiley & Sons, Ltd.

life possible. Students should think about the relative emphasis they put on learning skills for a job, on preparing for graduate education, and on pursuing the liberal arts. (See Chapter 15, "What To Do with a Bachelor of Arts in English.")

Part of college preparation is figuring out what it will cost. The elite colleges are the most heavily endowed, but other schools may offer a particular student a more generous financial aid package in order to attract him or her for either athletics or academic study. Taking enormous loans to attend an elite college may be a less desirable path than going to an in-state college. In the next chapter, I will be discussing in detail the cost issues.

What Parents Can Do

As soon as a child is born, parents should if possible begin to save funds for college. Many states give tax benefits to those who do so under 529 plans. It is reasonable for parents to ask their children – both while in high school and while attending college – to earn some money to contribute to the costs of college. But parents should not ask their children to sacrifice their schoolwork and – if it is at all economically feasible – their participation in school activities. Working during summers will give students valuable experience, while providing them with an opportunity to earn funds to help pay for college.

The more positive the home environment, the more likely a child will succeed in school. Reading to children at an early age teaches them the joy and importance of reading and stimulates intellectual curiosity. When parents take an interest in their children's day-to-day learning in school, children respond. But interest does not mean doing, and children need to learn to do their own work and turn to parents only after they have made a strong effort on their own. Not every parent will be able to help with advanced high school math and physics, but those who can help should focus on teaching the concepts rather than solving the problems.

Preparation for college should begin early. Parents need to play a motivating role, and we know that educated parents are more likely to produce educated children. But we also know that successful students – and those who in ensuing years make a significant difference in their fields – come from every socioeconomic and ethnic background, and that emphasis on learning within homes can take place even in difficult economic circumstances and urban neighborhoods with pervasive social problems. When first-generation college students succeed, we all succeed; they are evidence that the American dream – with its ideals of a meritocracy and opportunity for all – is working.

Amanda First, Cornell '12, observes:

A lot of public schools have a system of tracking, where they place you in mostly honors or mostly "college prep" (which is non-honors) classes before you even enter high school. It's important for parents and students to realize if they want the student to apply to an elite college, an honors track offers the most support, and [parents] should talk to eighth-grade teachers to find the best approaches to get on an honors track.

It is important that all parents, including those from diverse ethnic and socio-economic backgrounds, are fully aware of the available programs and resources. It is the responsibility of the school district as well as the parents to be sure this happens.

There are many ways parents can influence their children's success in school. Parents should monitor how their children spend their time, and they can begin this monitoring at a very early age. They need to be alert to their children's mental and physical health, and to face head-on issues of depression, learning disabilities, and physical limitation. They need to be aware of the people with whom their children spend time. If parents smoke, drink, and/or abuse drugs, they should rethink their behavior because their children are far more likely to imitate their choices.

Parents should stress the pleasures of reading – the exaltation of reading a great book – and insist on quiet time, as well as on a set number of TV hours and computer game hours per week. Parents can expose their children to cultural opportunities such as theater, music, museums, etc. If these are not readily available, trips to even small cities can complement the world of rural villages and towns. Even modest after-school enrichment programs can be helpful. Often communities work with school systems to offer financial help to poor families who might otherwise not be able to afford cultural events and enrichment programs for their children.

While parents should encourage participation in sports and the development of specific skills in the sports that children choose, they should also make their children aware of how few people earn their living as professional athletes. Being the best player on a high school team usually does not result in earning a livelihood in a sport.

Secondary Schools

High schools have different cultures, and those that focus on academic achievement usually best prepare students for selective universities. For students attending average high schools, even more of the motivation must come from within themselves and from their families.

Becca Harrison, Cornell '14, comments:

> I had very few high school teachers with any degree of confidence in my abilities, not to mention the limited opportunity for college-prep classes prior to Cornell (I spent my "free" time watching free lectures from MIT's Open Courseware site) – in fact, I'm not really sure where my motivation came from.

In some areas, if the situation demands it, parents can enroll their children in public schools with more favorable learning cultures than in those schools closest to their home. If this is not possible and funds permit, parents can look into private schools, some of which do offer scholarships to those in need.

Some high schools give students major advantages in college preparation and in the admission process. But the elite colleges seek geographic and ethnic diversity and want to accept students from all over the country. Magnet Schools, special public schools that select students by means of a rigorous test, are exceptionally qualified to prepare students for elite colleges. They include Stuyvesant, Hunter, and the Bronx High School of Science in New York, Boston Latin, Classical High School in Providence, the School for the Talented and Gifted in Dallas, and the Thomas Jefferson High School for Science and Technology in Annandale, Virginia. Other alternatives are elite private boarding schools such as Exeter, Choate, or Andover, or private day schools such as Dalton, Horace Mann, or Fieldston, in New York; the National Cathedral School in DC; Germantown Friends School in Philadelphia; and Harvard-Westlake School in Los Angeles.

Wherever you attend high school, finding a mentor – someone who, in addition to your family, is interested in your intellectual and personal growth – among your high school teachers or even outside the classroom is pivotal.

Writing of her own experience, Roya Sabra, Cornell '16, gives sound advice:

> [I]f attending a top private school is not a viable option, I would suggest looking critically at what public schools offer in academics, possible mentors, and extra-curricular activities. Students should look past a high school's reputation to pursue a good education.
>
> I was focused on science in middle and high school. I decided to attend my local public high school because I found a teacher who was a dedicated mentor in the classroom and for extra-curricular science activities such as science fair and ocean science bowl. A few of my friends from middle school had taken her classes and had decided to pursue science activities with her. They had chosen to attend the public school instead of a nearby private preparatory academy because of this teacher. After meeting her, I decided that the public high school was the right place for me. There, I entered a great learning community.

Though my high school doesn't have the best academic reputation overall, this mentor fostered an incredible, though relatively small, learning community.

I think it's important to look at potential secondary schools just as you would a college, considering how your interests and passions can be met by the resources and guidance the high school offers.

Though I didn't pursue science in college, finding a mentor to direct my passion during high school was vital to my continued love for learning.

What Students Can Do

It is never too early to think about what kind of career you want to have and to begin learning what kind of preparation that career will require. With the variety of colleges available, the rise in the cost of college, and the rapidly changing economy in the face of technological shifts and developments, students need to be savvy consumers and be as sure as possible that they are making choices that serve their interests and fulfill their goals. These choices include the college they attend, the majors and minors they pursue, the courses they take, and the skills they develop in classes and in extra-curricular activities. As much as circumstances permit, *you* need to shape your education.

Speaking to people about their careers and reading about how people earn livings are ways to develop a sense of what is right for you. If you are fortunate, your work will bring you joy and satisfaction. Knowing whether you want to be a doctor, lawyer, engineer, business executive, CPA, teacher, or college professor may help shape your high school curriculum and your choice of colleges, but developing the skills I mention below will be helpful to whatever career you choose.

It is good to have a career goal in mind in high school, even if it is tentative and subject to change as you develop and your goals and interests evolve. Many students change direction in college, but a career goal can motivate your commitment to your studies. While parents can set goals and serve as career models, you need to choose your own career path.

To succeed in higher education, you need to develop the skills of time management and disciplined study habits as early as middle school. It is a good idea to keep track in writing or in a computer file of how you are using your time. You need to set aside specific times for study; during those times you should turn off the TV and put the smartphone away. Realistically, you might begin with 30- to 40-minute study periods, but by your later high school years you should be able to concentrate without a break for at least 60 to 90 minutes.

The best preparation for college is to learn how to read carefully and thoroughly, whether it be fiction or non-fiction; the latter category includes newspapers in print or online. Select your reading with discrimination and rely on suggestions from teachers and other knowledgeable adults. In addition, it is important that you keep up with national and international news and issues and that you develop an interest in the world in which you live, including the rapidly changing world of science. Reading the *New York Times*, the best news source in the US, for at least a half-hour daily will help.

Reading well means reading skeptically and learning to recognize articles in newspapers or online where arguments are not logical or require more information. Developing a critical intelligence is a crucial component of learning.

Equally important to reading intelligently is developing your writing skills. That means taking every writing assignment seriously. It means learning to write drafts, and that requires beginning assignments as soon as they are given. Term papers can teach you how to do research and to use the library and Internet as research tools.

Writing well takes practice. Keeping a journal or diary – and being self-conscious about your prose, including correct grammar, sentence variety, and vocabulary development – is a good way to practice writing. I would buy (and read once a year) Strunk and White's *The Elements of Style*.

You also need to develop listening skills in class, and that means getting enough sleep. Taking notes in class will help you to develop listening skills and to organize material; the latter is essential not only for test taking but also for understanding any subject. If you are permitted to bring a laptop computer to class, take notes on that. Keep a separate file for each course and continue to re-organize your files as the semester progresses. Remember that you can always trim material if you write down too much, but you cannot recoup material that you have forgotten. If you miss class, borrowing another student's notes is essential, but always be sure to borrow from top students.

In an increasingly computer-centric and tech-savvy world, you need to know something about how the web works, regardless of your projected college major or career path. Most high schools now provide courses in technical skills. Acquiring these skills in high school – including basic HTML and CSS – can add value to almost any kind of CV as well as job or college application.

Finally, and this needs to be stressed, you need to develop verbal skills and learn to play a significant role in class discussion. You should speak in class even if it takes effort. Think of your class contributions as relatively important events. Participating in class discussion and responding to the ideas of others can help you clarify your thoughts for written assignments.

Making notes to yourself about what you want to say before you raise your hand helps many students overcome reluctance to speak in class. Not only in class, but even in conversation, try to eliminate "mmm"s, "you know"s, and "like"s when you speak.

Can Students Learn How to Learn Better?

To prepare for college, you need to think of high school as a challenge and an opportunity. Working hard is the best preparation. Curiosity, desire for knowledge, and the ability to solve complex, thought-provoking problems are important life skills. Conscientious students need also to be skeptical, innovative, and imaginative; really distinguished thinking, even in high school, comes from questioning what one is told, reading further in classroom topics, and, on occasion, going beyond accepted formulations as they are presented. This does not mean that you will discover a new theorem in math or a new element in chemistry, but it does mean that you will learn something about the process of discovery and the value of thinking outside the box.

Studying well is a matter of learning how to concentrate and block out everything else. Most people do better when not listening to music, but some people do seem to benefit from listening to soothing music when studying. Using study halls and homeroom periods to study, rather than wasting time on video games or social media, is a good way to be time efficient.

When it is permitted, studying with a classmate can be helpful, but you must choose your study partner wisely and keep focused on the work at hand and not on other matters. Indeed, choice of friends is an important ingredient of school success, and if your social group is motivated to learn, the chances are better that you too will be.

Take challenging courses, including basic sciences and math, even if those are not your primary interest. Struggling to keep up and learning from mistakes are part of how we grow in school, in our avocations (music, sports, etc.), and in life.

In computing a student's class rank and grade point average (GPA), many high schools give extra points for advanced and honors courses. If you can do the work in these courses, take them. Be alert that some local colleges offer Advanced Placement courses that are not available in less competitive high schools. Colleges consider the difficulty of high school programs when weighing students' applications. Equally important for you, succeeding in difficult courses will be the best preparation for the next educational challenges.

Success breeds success. While academic success is hardly the only predictor of career success, there is a correlation between them. Having said that, I should mention that I have had some students make a conscious choice to focus as much or more on acting in theatre groups or writing for the *Cornell Daily Sun* than on academics. By doing so they have put themselves on their chosen career path; sometimes these choices begin in high school. However, devoting oneself to athletics at the expense of school is usually a mistake given that so few athletes succeed professionally.

No matter what your interests and career goals, you must not neglect math and science. (You might read Steven Strogatz's *The Joy of X*.) Without high school biology, chemistry, physics, college preparatory math and/or calculus as well as computer science, you will be much less able to understand the world in which you live. Furthermore, by not taking such classes, you foreclose some of your future options in pursuing sciences and engineering. Moreover, colleges expect you to have basic knowledge in these areas, even if you ultimately study the humanities, social sciences, or a business curriculum.

Even now when English is becoming the basic language of the world, it is important to study a foreign language. For one thing, it will help you understand the world better because you will learn something about another culture. You will be preparing yourself for more possible choices if you decide to do a junior year – or junior semester – abroad as well as for more future career opportunities.

Be alert about who are the best teachers, and take advice on who they are from the best students. Great teachers are demanding in terms of standards, but also create an environment where students experience learning as a privilege and a pleasure. Getting to know some of your teachers well will give you the necessary sources of recommendations for your applications. Getting to know the advisor or guidance counselor who prepares the material transmitted to college is essential.

Other Suggestions

Participate in extra-curricular activities such as varsity sports, the school newspaper, drama and choral groups, orchestra and band, debating, and student government. Developing skills and competence in these areas builds self-confidence. High school is more rewarding, fulfilling, and fun for those who are part of the school community. Moreover, selective colleges favor for admission those who play leadership roles in such activities; colleges do so in part because leaders, at a more advanced level, play a vital role in college life and in part because the best advertisements for a college are alumni who have leadership roles in their communities and on the state and national levels.

College admissions departments are also favorably impressed with applicants who volunteer in the community beyond school by tutoring children or reading to those adults who for various reasons cannot read, working with the disabled, or giving some time at the local hospital or hospice. Volunteerism can be connected with your church, synagogue, mosque, or other religious institution. Meaningful summer and after-school paid jobs, such as working as a counselor for younger children or in a hospital lab, are also seen as a plus by those deciding admission. But the more important reason to volunteer or take jobs is that doing so will enlarge your perspective and create experiences that will enrich your life now and later.

As Juliana Hughes, Cornell '17, suggests:

> I think that perhaps there is a danger in emphasizing the college application over what some of the skills and activities will give back to the student later in his life. For example, volunteering at a hospital does provide excellent college résumé material, but the student should do meaningful things that both appeal to him and are impressive on his résumé – he should not volunteer at a hospital simply because Cornell [or some other elite college] will accept him!

Nothing is more important in adolescence than physical and mental health. Getting a full night's sleep, eating properly with minimal junk food and fast food, and avoiding cigarettes, drugs, and alcoholic beverages will enhance your enjoyment of life and your success in your studies. Regular exercise, whether it be as part of a high school team or on your own, is essential.

No matter how dedicated you are to a project, you need to take some time for fun activities. Each day you need to do something you like, whether it be a walk, a visit to a museum, watching your favorite TV show, or pursuing a hobby.

Conclusion

Standardized tests such as the SAT and the ACT play an important role in admission. Competitive public high schools and private schools often offer on-site preparation for these tests. Some parents either pay for outside special classes or hire a private tutor.

In the spring and summer of your junior year, you should begin to visit campuses in which you are interested. However, even earlier you should begin learning about what colleges are for you. Interview processes vary, but they seem to play less of a role than they once did. Most public universities have dropped them; the select private colleges and universities rely on alumni interviews, but, in my experience on Cornell admission committees, these interviews are not much of a factor in admissions.

Although the college application and admission procedure is stressful, it is important to remember that discovering the joy and privilege of learning in high school and college is much more important than where you do your undergraduate work.

3

The College Olympics: How to Choose the Right College and How to Get the Right College to Choose You

Introduction

Finding the right fit for college is a complex process requiring considerable effort. But, because most colleges now accept the Common Application, it is much easier than it once was to apply to several colleges at once.

Keep in mind that the very low percentage of students admitted to some elite schools has been artificially inflated by students applying to a larger number of colleges. (My own preference would be to limit the number of applications to eight or so, but that is not likely to happen.)

If you are a top student with strong SAT or ACT scores, you have a good chance of being admitted to an elite college even if the college is not necessarily your first choice. Kevin Carey puts these numbers in perspective in his November 29, 2014 *New York Times* article entitled "For Accomplished Students, Reaching a Good College Isn't as Hard as It Seems":

> Enabled by technology that makes it easier to copy and send electronic documents and driven by the competitive anxiety that plummeting admission rates produce, top students have been sending out more applications. ... It turns out that four out of five well-qualified students who apply to elite schools are accepted by at least one. These numbers come courtesy of Parchment.com, a website that helps students submit college transcripts electronically and navigate the applications and admissions world.

How to Succeed in College and Beyond: The Art of Learning, First Edition. Daniel R. Schwarz.
© 2016 John Wiley & Sons, Ltd. Published 2016 by John Wiley & Sons, Ltd.

The College Olympics: How to Choose the Right College

In his best-selling *Where You Go Is Not Who You'll Be: An Antidote to the College Admissions Mania* (2015), Frank Bruni rightly stresses that where you go to college is less important than what you make of that experience. But I do see value in going to a college or university where you will be challenged by an accomplished peer group with a zeal for learning and by professors who demand excellence.

I agree with the observation of Jonathan Landman, former deputy managing editor for the *New York Times*, in an email to me that most students will be admitted to the appropriate tier or what he calls "band":

> I've always thought that the choice of a college is the single most overrated decision in anybody's life. This bizarre preoccupation over whether somebody goes to this or that Ivy, or that or this liberal arts college is such a waste of energy. Because of course it doesn't make a whit of difference. It's not as if a kid is going to be faced with a choice between Harvard and Hostos Community College. You qualify in a certain band where the alternatives are more or less comparable.

It is worth paying some attention to college rankings, including the much publicized *US News & World Report*, but, as Ronald G. Ehrenberg has pointed out in his excellent book *Tuition Rising: Why College Costs So Much*, the criteria vary, and in some cases colleges make decisions that affect their rankings more than their actual quality (50–69). Be aware that you are looking for the right place for *you*.

You should know that the College Olympics competition is not always fair. Legacies – that is, children and grandchildren of those who have graduated – may be given preference. Those whose families are big donors will probably be given even more preference. Other beneficiaries of affirmative action are faculty and staff children. Some weight is also given to local applicants whose parents are not directly employed by the college.

Athletes are given preferential treatment; this is the case even at schools like the Ivies which do not offer athletic scholarships, but do find places for applicants – especially those who will play major sports – who might not otherwise be admitted. To be more precise, the Ivies and some of the elite Division Three schools – Emory, Williams, Amherst, Middlebury, among others – offer need-based scholarships for accepted athletes, using the same formula as for other students.

The emphasis on social, ethnic, and economic diversity does mean that some students will be admitted whose credentials are comparable to others who will be turned down. But we need to remember that other applicants also may have advantages. Many applicants from economically comfortable backgrounds have had in-school and expensive private coaching on taking SAT and ACT tests and even on writing the required application essays. Some go to

25

private schools or highly sophisticated suburban public schools that have counselors and teachers who are savvy in knowing how to present their candidates; these counselors and teachers know how to write letters recommending their students and even how to best fill in the boxes indicating to which percentiles a student belongs in terms of ability, character, and potential. The person in charge of the school's college admissions may have a special relationship with a particular college's admissions department.

Reading admissions folders in spring 2015 and in the past, I am struck by the difference in the quality of submitted student essays. Some applicants hurt themselves by essays that were not proofread, while others wrote silly stuff that a teacher or guidance person should have vetted. There is nothing wrong with asking a teacher – in most cases, your English teacher – to read a draft of your college application before submitting it.

In some cases, the recommendations from the school, including teachers' letters, left something to be desired in terms of depth and clarity. Teachers need to know that when writing letters of recommendation, the genre requires enthusiasm if not hyperbole. They need to ask themselves if the candidate deserves to be admitted, and if the answer is yes, they need to write the necessary letter to give the applicant a chance.

(1) Find a match between your interests and the schools you apply to. You need to decide whether you prefer a rural or urban environment, whether distance from home is important, whether you wish to go to a school that foregrounds your particular religion, whether the size of the enrollment matters, and whether you want a true campus experience where students live on campus and near classrooms.

There has always been a difference between a research university and a small liberal arts college. Research universities stress developing new knowledge, while colleges stress teaching what is known to students. But the line has blurred, and at the more elite small colleges and at many universities that are not known as major research universities, substantive research is carried on, while teachers at major universities are encouraged more than in the past to be competent teachers.

You want to learn about the size of classes, whether they are taught by senior faculty or adjunct faculty and/or teaching assistants, and whether undergraduates – especially in the sciences and engineering but also in the social sciences and the humanities – have a chance to do advanced research. You might also think about the physical facilities and resources that are available. You wouldn't go to the University of Florida if snow skiing were an important part of your life.

(2) Find a match between your high school record and abilities and the schools to which you apply. You can find out whether your grades, rank in class, and SAT and/or ACT scores meet the qualifications of the schools that interest you. Standard tests are a way that colleges get data that shows them whether an A in one school equals an A in another. But some diligent and creative students do not test well and are therefore at a disadvantage. While tutoring or enrollment in private classes can bridge the testing problem, they are not guarantees to more successful college applications, in part because so many people do some kind of test preparation. Indeed, in some communities even those who test well on preliminary SATs and ACTSs take such courses.

Be aware that the writing component of applications is taken very seriously at the competitive schools. Keep in mind that what is funny to a 17 year old is rarely funny to those reading applications. Ask your English teacher and/or guidance counselor to read over the written material you are submitting. Be aware of such technical errors as comma splices and dependent clauses after a semi-colon. Carefully proofread the final draft on the Common Application. Keep in mind that on the school-specific supplement, you can make a case that you are an excellent candidate for a particular school.

Presumably in your freshman year of high school you began the process of learning what courses are necessary and have taken the courses that you need to apply to specific colleges. If you are thinking of elite colleges or universities (and what is elite is debatable) – or, indeed, any of the flagship campuses of four-year state colleges, many of which have select programs for their best students – you should have taken honors and Advanced Placement courses.

When we think of elite and selective schools, we think of such schools as the Ivies, MIT, Caltech, Stanford, Duke, the University of Chicago, Northwestern, Johns Hopkins, and many of our great state universities like Berkeley, UCLA, Virginia, Michigan, Indiana, Wisconsin, Illinois, and Texas, along with quite a number of smaller private colleges from Amherst, Williams, Bowdoin, and Middlebury in the Northeast to Reed and the five Claremont colleges out West. But we also need to think of such excellent if slightly less prestigious and often less costly universities – especially for in-state residents – as (to name a few) Binghamton and Buffalo of the New York State system, the University of Vermont, the University of Oregon, the University of Maryland, and Penn State. (A useful website is College Confidential). However, because the elite colleges and universities have more scholarship funds, they may be actually less expensive than the sticker price of the seemingly less expensive schools.

In the application process, note that extra-curricular activities and community service matter. But it is better to excel in and/or play a leadership role in one or two activities than to be a participant in a long list.

For non-elite schools, you should investigate the graduation rate and the time from matriculation to commencement.

(3) Find a match between the anticipated costs and your ability to pay. Keep in mind that lifetime earnings soar with a bachelor's degree and continue to soar with a master's and doctorate. Although earnings vary with field and college, what Ronald G. Ehrenberg wrote in 2000 is still true: "Numerous studies indicate that the economic gains of students from attending selective private institutions, both as undergraduates and as graduate professional degree students, are substantial" (*Tuition Rising*, 5). But be somewhat wary of surveys about which colleges produce the highest income for its students. For instance, in an email to me of February 27, 2015, Ehrenberg cautions against taking seriously PayScale's 2014–15 College Salary Report: "This nonsystematic survey shows earnings; it does not say anything about [actual costs to students and parents]. And it does not control for the fact that the people with the highest income earning potential are the ones who get admitted to the best places."

Learn what kind of financial aid is available to you and whether that aid takes the form of scholarships, work study jobs, other jobs, or loans. You should begin by filling out the Free Application for Federal Student Aid, or FAFSA. State and college sponsored aid programs usually rely on this form. While colleges use this to put together aid packages, usually with a mix of grants, work study, and loans, these will vary depending on the financial conditions of the colleges and whether they want to include a merit component as a way of inducing you to enroll. In some instances, especially if you are offered different packages by different colleges, you can ask if your package can be increased (see Ann Carrns, "How to Appeal College Financial Aid Offers").

Before borrowing, students receiving Federal student loans are required to have counseling sessions. Most colleges use online modules that the Federal Education Department supplies. But be aware that these modules are not as clear and simple as they might be and require considerable financial acumen to understand (see Ron Lieber, "Navigating the Thickets of Student Loan Counseling").

Be aware, too, that some colleges have eliminated need-blind admission. As Ron Lieber writes in his May 16, 2014 *New York Times* article "A Beginner's Guide to Repaying Student Loans":

> Since the Great Recession, the list of colleges that have eliminated need-blind admissions has grown ever longer. Reed, Wesleyan, Tufts, Colby, Agnes Scott and ... Clark University are among those that no longer make all of their admissions decisions without looking at financial information, and a family's ability to pay. Taking into consideration tuition, room and board, travel costs, and funds for miscellaneous costs, make up budgets for the colleges that interest you.

There is an increasing and commendable awareness of the soaring costs of higher education and there have been many proposals to reduce those costs, such as President Obama's proposal that two years of community college be free. But do understand that until proposals become law and/or Federal or State government policy, they are just ideas.

How much debt you should incur depends on many factors, including your expected future earnings, but be careful about mortgaging your future. You need to understand the terms of your loans and repayment protocols (Lieber, "A Beginner's Guide to Repaying Student Loans").

It may take some time to research loan programs and repayment protocols. Be aware that income-driven repayment programs may affect your monthly payment and that if you work full-time in a public service position, you may qualify for the Public Service Loan Forgiveness Program (see Federal Student Aid). According to a February 10, 2015 *New York Times* article by Kevin Carey:

> A growing number of people are enrolling in a federal program called Income-Based Repayment (I.B.R.) to pay back their college loans. I.B.R. limits monthly loan payments to as little as 10 percent of a borrower's income, after deductions for living expenses, and forgives any remaining loan balances after 20 years. People who work in nonprofit and public-sector jobs get an even better deal, with forgiveness after 10 years.

In past decades, especially the 1970s and 1980s, because of high inflation, students were repaying loans more easily. That is, the dollar they borrowed was worth much more than the dollar they repaid. But this has not been the case for some years. Now fixed interest rates are lower than they have been and that makes repayment somewhat easier as long as you borrow an amount that you can pay back.

How will you pay for college if your parents cannot afford it or are unwilling to pay for most or all of it? The latter problem is sometimes fixed by legally declaring yourself to be an independent adult without supporting family, in which cases your aid will be based on your own earnings and assets (see FinAid); be forewarned that this process is not easy.

The good news for those families of modest means is that a sustained effort is being made to help low-income high achievers get the necessary financial support to thrive in college. Whether this effort at economic diversity will succeed depends in part on whether the colleges themselves will sacrifice tuition revenue in the interests of economic diversity. As David Leonardt points out in his October 28, 2014 *New York Times* article "A New Push to Get Low-Income Students Through College": "On some campuses, including Caltech, Dartmouth, Notre Dame and Washington University in St. Louis, fewer than 15 percent of entering students receive federal Pell grants, which go roughly to students from the bottom two-fifths of the income distribution." One problem is that supporting economic diversity depends on the school's endowment, and those with lower endowments per student have fewer resources.

While state universities will often cost less, especially for residents, the disparity between resident and non-resident tuition is disappearing. As Kevin Carey notes in his May 18, 2015 *New York Times* article "The In-State Tuition Break, Slowly Disappearing":

> Many of the most elite public universities are steadily restricting the number of students who are allowed to pay in-state tuition. ... A result is the creeping privatization of elite public universities that have historically provided an accessible route to jobs in academia, business and government. One of the most important paths to upward mobility, open on a meritocratic basis to people from all economic classes, is narrowing. ...
>
> Instead of extending their traditional mission of providing an affordable, high-quality education to local residents, [elite public] universities focused on recruiting students from other states and nations, many of whom paid much higher tuition rates. As a result, the number of in-state spots relative to the college-going population as a whole declined significantly at national public universities.

But some encouraging news is that many of the elite colleges – including all the Ivies – do need-blind admissions and have the resources to help those whom they admit and who need financial assistance. You should not be scared off by the "sticker price" of even the most expensive private colleges because there are means of getting significant support. Also, many schools offer merit scholarships to attract top students. The more highly endowed schools will offer an aid package with a large grant component. Other good news is that the US Department of Education has the Pell Grant program to help fund college education, although the maximum 2014–15 grant is only $5,730. For the Ivy League and other schools with comparatively large endowments, qualification for the Pell is a signal to schools to provide – in almost all cases – generous aid packages. Further good news is that there are many other scholarship programs, including those restricted to residents in each state; in New York State these range from $500 to $1,500. In addition, there are many private scholarships administered by such organizations as the Rotary, although the latter focuses on study abroad.

Cornell does not have the financial resources of Harvard, Yale, Princeton, or Stanford. Yet, in the Cornell class of 2017, consisting of 3,261 students, 47.8 percent were eligible for need-based aid and 44.4 percent received need-based aid from Cornell sources, averaging $35,735 in grant aid – which does not have to be repaid – and $5,783 in loans. These figures will vary. Thus the class of 2018 had a slightly lower percentage of students receiving aid but a higher dollar amount.

It is true that Harvard, with its more than $37 billion endowment shielded from taxes as a non-profit educational institution, could be even more generous and that would result in a more economically and socially diverse student body. Unlike foundations, colleges and universities do not have to spend 5 percent of their endowment's capital. As Ron Unz has remarked in his March 31, 2015 *New York Times* article "End Tuition at Elite Colleges to Attract More Applicants": "If all of Harvard's college students disappeared tomorrow, or attended classes without paying a dime, the financial impact on Harvard, Inc. would be completely negligible." Yale, Princeton, and Stanford are in a similar position and there are probably several others, including some of the highly endowed smaller colleges.

Another source of scholarships is athletics, but be aware that neither the Ivies nor the (usually) smaller colleges in Division Three offer athletic scholarships. Be aware, too, that many more parents think that their children are candidates for athletic scholarships than there are scholarships and that Division One scholarships often have expectations for practice, conditioning, travel, and competition that take significant time from studies. New rulings seem to allow some schools to give more aid than in the past, but at what price to the student?

In addition, there are various loan programs, although I am wary of loans that saddle young people with enormous debts that can affect their ability to buy a home, start a family, choose a low-paying career such as social work or elementary and secondary school teaching, as well as prepare for retirement. In fact, a handful of top universities have eliminated loans from aid packages. I expect more to follow.

Avoid for-profit colleges, many of which have engaged in fraudulent practices and are responsible for a disproportionate amount of student loan defaults. Several government studies have exposed these schools as taking advantage of gullible students and making exaggerated claims.

(4) One key to college success is finding professors who are interested in you; it is worth researching whether teaching and mentoring are stressed at the colleges to which you apply. Before you decide where to apply, the more you can learn about the school and the departments and professors that interest you, the better.

Both small colleges and large universities have great teachers, but the latter will have more courses taught and graded by graduate students who may also serve in science courses as lab instructors. On the other hand, research universities will offer a wider variety of courses and programs.

Is it better, you might ask, to work with a world-class scholar at a top research university who opens the doors to exciting and complex projects and ideas than with a capable, enthusiastic professor who does little or no research? Or are you more likely to find at an excellent small college a professor who challenges you and shows interest in your growth as a person?

There is no one answer, but in my experience you are just as likely to find the ideal mentor at a large university as at a small college. Katherine Burroughs, Cornell '85, recalls: "What is really remarkable, though, is not with standing the size of [Cornell] and the focus on being a research institution, I can count on a few fingers the *bad* experiences."

Keep in mind that major research universities can offer students opportunities to work with senior scholars on grants and thus give you a leg up for graduate school. There are programs like Cornell's Presidential Research Scholars that enable students to do independent research under the auspices of a senior scholar; these programs are not limited to the sciences but can include the humanities.

My sense is that teaching at research universities, including teaching in STEM (science, technology, engineering, and mathematics) courses, has improved dramatically in recent decades. At research universities, teaching effectiveness is not only more of a component in tenure decisions, but also stressed more in the administration's review of a department's and individual's performances than used to be the case.

Because of a tight job market, professors trained at the strongest graduate programs are everywhere now, and you will be able to find excellent mentors not only at the most selective colleges and flagship state universities, but at almost any college, including community colleges.

(5) Suggestions #1–#4 mean that you need to do the necessary research. This means allotting time to do some reading in catalogues and online sites – and, if possible, speaking to people attending the colleges that interest you. Talk not only to your guidance counselor or the person handling college applications, but also to teachers whom you respect.

(6) Visiting colleges is a good idea, but don't overestimate what you learn in a campus visit. The best visits are overnight ones during the week that include living in the dorms and attending classes rather than visits on football weekends, particularly at schools where football means that partying is foregrounded.

If you are a prospective athlete, you will meet the coach, and if he or she is interested in you as a potential player, you may be recruited with tales of championships and even exposed to campus partying, especially on weekends. You need to look at athletic facilities, find out how likely you are to play, and if you are offered an athletic scholarship, find out whether you will lose it if you are injured or if you or the university decides you are not going to be on the team. You need to do some research into whether the school is using you to bolster its athletic reputation or if it is really interested in your getting an education. There has been ample evidence that some universities are not educating many of their top athletes, especially in visible and revenue-earning sports.

The worst reason to go to any college is because you think there will be lots of partying – whether revolving around teams on which you play, the Greek system, or the campus culture – and sometimes 18-year-olds forget this.

(7) Early decision (which is binding if the college accepts you and usually requires an application in November) and early action (which does not require a commitment until the regular commitment deadline of May 1) are often good options. In many elite schools these early applications give you a better chance of being admitted. For either, you apply to only one school. Early action still gives you a chance to apply elsewhere later and compare financial aid offers. However, if you choose the early decision path, you cannot compare financial aid packages; for those needing aid, early decision may not be the best alternative.

In my limited experience on admission committees at Cornell's College of Arts and Sciences, those deferred during the early admission process do not usually get admitted later. Nor are many students admitted from the so-called wait list. My guess is that this is true at virtually all the select schools, and if you are deferred or waitlisted, you need to find out the facts on these matters. Your slim chances of being admitted off the wait list are increased by writing an enthusiastic letter to the school expressing your strong interest, but don't become a nuisance by frequently writing and calling.

(8) For those taking part in the regular application process or those who are rejected or deferred in the early decision or early action process, "safety schools"– those whom research plus your guidance counselor suggest are likely to admit you – are a good way to avoid disappointment. How many schools you should apply to depends on your qualifications and the competitiveness of the schools to which you are applying. Those seeking admission to elite schools are applying to more schools than in the past (see Ariel Kaminer, "Applications by the Dozen, as Anxious Seniors Hedge College Bets"). One advantage of doing so is that the financial packages offered by the schools that admit you may vary and be a factor in your final choice.

(9) Think of the college admission process as an Olympic event in which you do your best, but if you don't get admitted where you want to be, be a good sport and realize this is NOT a judgment on your life to date or your potential. In other words, you must not take rejection as a defeat. *What* you do at college is far more important than *where* you do it.

Frank Bruni (*Where You Go*) and others have written about the panic and hysteria some families associate with this process, although in most cases I would use terms like "mild anxiety" and "moderate neuroses" to describe responses that are mostly much less severe than the severe symptoms that these authors describe.

Certainly, some parents in well-to-do urban and suburban areas pay exorbitant fees to professionals to help their children in the application procedure and are in a state for months if not years about whether their children will go to an elite college. But the vast majority of parents take the application process in their stride and keep in mind that their children will survive this process and move on to the next challenge, namely doing their best wherever they end up going.

What is wonderful, remarkable, and really needs to be stressed is that when students arrive at the place that has accepted them and they have chosen to attend – whether it be Cornell, Bucknell, or the University of Wyoming – they throw themselves into the experience and don't look backwards. Indeed, most if not all of the students' angst during the application/admission Olympics – and, in most cases, that of their parents – dissolves rather rapidly once they know where they are going.

(10) Once you have made a choice, commit yourself fully to that choice rather than think about "would haves" and "should haves" or what might have been.

(11) Transferring is a possibility – and some schools give students "guaranteed transfer" if they meet certain stipulations – but in most cases the best thing is to give your all to the school in which you enroll. If you are doubtful about which field you want to go into, choose a larger university with many choices of fields in which to major. That choice may be more important in STEM, because you are preparing for a specific career, than it is in the liberal arts, where your skills in reading, writing, thinking analytically, making oral presentations, and summoning evidence are most important; in some liberal arts fields, you can move readily from one area to another. (See Chapter 13, "Why Study the Humanities?")

In general, it is easier to transfer from science and engineering programs into liberal arts than vice versa. If you are interested in STEM, it is best to start in STEM.

(12) One way for some students to save on costs is to apply to a Canadian university or a university abroad. Canadian universities often do not require standard test scores or recommendations or essays – and some only require senior grades – but they do give preference to students in their province (see Lynn O'Shaughnessy, "10 Reasons to Attend Canadian Universities"). Canadian students submit their application to an application service or to the university and list their preference order.

At Queen's University, one of Canada's elite schools, an American student's costs for tuition plus room and board might be in the neighborhood of two-thirds of an elite American school. Not only are there merit scholarships for international students, but you can also still apply for loans offered by the US government under the Federal Stafford loans program and PLUS loans programs.

Universities in countries other than Canada are also possible choices and will be less costly than the most expensive US universities. British universities require the Universities and College Admissions Service Application (see Complete University Guide, "Applying to British University" and Rebecca R. Ruiz, "Applying to College in the United Kingdom").

Only Oxford and Cambridge require applicant interviews; both welcome but do not require SAT and ACT test scores. For Oxford and Cambridge, an essay is also required but it is, rather than a personal essay, one focusing on your academic plans.

Obviously, you need to weigh costs – including scholarship support – and quality of education in making your decisions on whether going abroad for undergraduate education is for you.

Alternative Paths to a College Education

But there are many scenarios other than the college Olympics. Great teaching and mentoring can take place at community colleges and commuting four-year schools. When cost is an issue or when you are undecided about your direction, commuting to college can make a great deal of sense, and so can spending your first two college years getting an associate degree at a community college.

Some states have innovative programs for getting a college degree. For example, New York's Empire State College has a fully accredited program for associate and bachelor degrees which allows a combination of online and on-site courses and even gives college credit for certain kinds of work experience. Thomas Edison State College in New Jersey seems to offer credit for work experience, but for these alternative ways to get degrees you need to do careful research and be aware of scams.

Questions That Are Part of the Process for Many Young People

Is college for everyone? Do you want to go to college upon high school graduation or would it be better to go into the Armed Services (see Go Army) and go to college later when the Service will pay much of the costs? What if you have to work for some years to support a family? What if, because of financial reasons, you are thinking of going to college part-time? What if you didn't do so well in high school, but now, after working or military experience, you feel ready for college? What if you need, for family and personal reasons, to stay home?

For some students, the answers to the foregoing questions will lead to a decision to begin higher education at community colleges. Despite the focus in my earlier comments on "elite" and "selective" colleges, we need to remember almost half of US undergraduates are enrolled in community colleges and many more are in four-year commuter colleges; in both these categories of colleges, the road from high school matriculation to graduation can be difficult.

In "Community College Students Face a Very Long Road to Graduation," part of a *New York Times* series focusing on LaGuardia Community College in Queens, New York City, Gina Bellafonte writes:

> In recent years, mounting concerns about inequality have fixated on the need for greater economic diversity at elite colleges, but the interest has tended to obscure the fact that the vast majority of high school students – including the wealthiest – will never go to Stanford or the University of Chicago or Yale. Even if each of US News and World Report's 25 top-ranked universities committed to turning over all of its spots to poor students, the effort would serve fewer than 218,000 of them. Community colleges have 7.7 million students enrolled, 45 percent of all undergraduates in the country. ...
>
> More than 70 percent of LaGuardia students come from families with incomes of less than $25,000 a year. The college reports that 70 percent of its full-time students who graduated after six years transferred to four-year colleges, compared with just 18 percent nationally, but only a quarter of LaGuardia students received an associate degree within six years.

At times, students at community college do not have access to the mentors and counselors who understand the ins and outs of transferring to four-year schools. Moreover, many classes are taught by underpaid and overburdened adjuncts who may have little time for individual conferences because they have too many students or may even have another part-time (or full-time) job somewhere else. If you take this route, you need to educate yourself on these matters and, in the best case, find mentors among your teachers and advising deans who will help you.

My brother, Robert Schwarz, Dartmouth '65 and a retired journalist, teaches writing courses at Glendale Community College in the Phoenix, Arizona, area and enjoys his work even though the pay is low:

> I like the work. ... Adjunct teaching works for people retired from something else who want something purposeful to do. ... No one should underestimate the challenges and frustrations of teaching community college students, but they are well behaved if the teacher wants that to be the case, students usually work harder than they are expected to, and they often learn vastly more than they learned in Arizona high schools.

My sense from talking to people who teach at community colleges and from students I have met, some of whom have transferred to Cornell, is that many of them are eager to learn, have interesting backgrounds, and are willing to accept intellectual challenges.

My former Cornell English Department colleague the late Phillip Marcus, who later taught at a less selective four-year college, Florida International, eloquently reminded me in a late 2014 note that there is a world quite different from Cornell and other prestigious schools, a world in which professors face challenges that Ivy League and other elite schools can hardly imagine:

> My own experience for the past twenty years would be quite different from yours as 80 percent of our 60,000 students are minorities (Hispanic, African-American, Afro-Caribbean) and most of them come from poor families and almost all work part-time or even full-time while carrying full loads of classes. I always have students who can't afford the textbooks. ....
>
> My students here face so many daunting challenges just to afford to go, though our cost is about $50,000 lower per year than [Cornell]. ... As an example of differences between CU and FIU, the state mandates that we submit textbook orders very early, because a great number of our students simply cannot afford to buy new books and must search for used ones. Often the bargain books don't arrive in time and students are without books during the first crucial weeks of the semester.

To give another perspective that shows how difficult success at college can be for those marginally prepared, I cite a note to me from Wendy Yoder, Retention Coordinator at Southwestern Oklahoma State University, another non-elite four-year university:

> Southwestern is ... dedicated to students and willing to implement whatever changes necessary to optimize the success of our students. ... [W]e sometimes overlook the natural waning process that occurs between a freshman and senior class. College is not for everyone, but I believe that we can make a positive influence in the lives of our students even if they decide on another path in the future.

Despite these difficulties, four-year schools like Florida International and Southwestern Oklahoma, where many and, in some places, most students are commuters, provide a viable alternative to the more expensive colleges and offer students without great means and perhaps without honor grades in high school a chance to earn the necessary college degree to find a good job and make a difference in their communities.

Similarly, community colleges play a crucial role for a great many students. They are often feeder schools for state university systems and provide a resource for upward mobility. They offer associate degrees after two years of successful full-time study. But because many of their students work full-time and go to school part-time, progress can be slow. Indeed, far too many students drop out of classes during the term. Yet motivated students often thrive in these schools and, after finishing a four-year degree, go on to graduate school.

Conclusion

While not for everyone, higher education will not only expand your earning power by developing your skills and intellect, but also open the doors and windows to the pleasures of reading and the joy of learning.

Part II

The College Experience

4

Twenty Suggestions for Incoming College Freshmen

The following suggestions apply to all entering freshmen, although a few may be more apropos to those living on campus. Needless to say, this is far from an exhaustive list, but one that students, parents, and colleagues might think of as a point of departure.

Basics

(1) Keep your career and life goals in mind, and remember why you enrolled at the college and in the program you chose.

(2) College is an opportunity, but you need to be a savvy consumer; that means more than not wasting your own money or that of your parents as well as more than not running up loans beyond you and your parents' ability to repay. Being a savvy consumer means taking advantage of what is offered in terms of personal and intellectual growth as well as developing the necessary skills for the next stage of life. Savvy college consumers take advantage of opportunities and learn what resources are available, not only on campus in terms of courses, professors, extra-curricular activities, museums, theater, work, and volunteerism, but also within the community in which the campus is located.

(3) After a reasonable amount of time, if you and your academic program are not a good match, think about changing direction within

How to Succeed in College and Beyond: The Art of Learning, First Edition. Daniel R. Schwarz.
© 2016 John Wiley & Sons, Ltd. Published 2016 by John Wiley & Sons, Ltd.

the college or, if you are at a university, transferring to another college within that university. A "reasonable amount of time" is admittedly vague; when to change direction will vary from person to person. Student input has made me think that in most cases at least an entire academic year is more appropriate than one semester.

Yoshiko Toyoda, Cornell '14, counsels that students should be patient before changing fields:

> For many Science/Math/Engineering majors, a lot of freshman and sophomore classes are going to be laying foundations that may not be obviously related to your field. For example, all of my engineering friends had to first get through all of the differential equations and physics courses, which they may not have enjoyed, in order to fulfill the prerequisite to take upper-level, interesting, applied engineering courses.

You should take your time about transferring to another college or university unless the college to which you are transferring was always your first choice and you had been given "guaranteed transfer" if you met certain stipulations. Be sure you are not transferring just because you are being asked to meet higher standards than in high school or because you are not the center of attention that you were there.

Subin Chung, Cornell '15 and a transfer, advises:

> [A] student should probably take at least a year (rather than a semester) to judge whether they should transfer — one semester isn't enough. First semester is often just adjusting to change; second semester is when you really realize whether that particular school is the right fit for you.

Time Management

(4) If any one thing determines success in school and in life for people of comparable potential and ability, it is time management, that is, using time effectively and efficiently. Keep a daily record of how you are using your time; each evening, schedule the next day, even while knowing you won't be following that schedule exactly.

You need a regular routine for doing your academic work. When you awake, think about how the day will be going in terms of time, including how much time you will be spending on extra-curricular activities (varsity or club or intramural sports, university publications such as the school newspaper or literary magazine, band or orchestra), paid employment, community volunteering, and social activities.

Jenni Higgs, Cornell '01, suggests:

> [I]t might be helpful to encourage students to explore resources on campus that can help them adjust to new academic demands (e.g., study groups, counseling/ study centers, etc.). It might be comforting to freshmen to know that it's common to feel overwhelmed initially and that there are plenty of organizations on campus to help them through rough patches.

An important Basic Rule: no time period is too short to accomplish something, and sometimes – especially when writing about something that you have been thinking about for a while – the time constraints of 15 or 20 minutes can actually produce better results than longer time periods. It may be that in some cases if people have less time for a task, they are more efficient (see Kevin Daum, "8 Things Really Efficient People Do").

If you have time between classes, learn to use that time. If you have a 50-minute class at 9:05 that ends at 9:55 and another that begins at 11:15, use those 80 minutes productively.

Know that the week has 168 hours. Be aware of how much time you spend with your smartphone, email, and social media such as Facebook, Twitter, etc. Be aware, too, of how much time you spend on social activities.

I remember reading that in July 1718, Cotton Mather advised his son Samuel, as he was going off to college:

> My Dear Child, look on Idleness as no better than wickedness. Begin betimes to set a value upon time, very loathe to throw it away on impertinencies. You have but a little time to live; but by the truest wisdom from you may live much in a little time; every night think how have I spent my time today, and be grieved if you can't say, you have gotten or done some good in the day.

Mark Eisner, Cornell Ph.D. '70, who has been both a teacher and administrator at Cornell, and has also spent time in private industry, admonishes:

> In managing time, it is important to be aware, not just of a schedule, but of how productive you are able to be at each point in the schedule. All hours spent on tasks are not equivalent – if you are overtired it can take extra time to complete tasks, and if you miss a class or fall asleep during [the class], it can cost more time to catch up than it would have taken to be in class and attentive to the material. That extra time then gets stolen from other tasks, with the risk of falling further and further behind.

Zivah Perel, Cornell '99, who teaches at Queensborough Community College, CUNY (The City University of New York), reminds us of the differences between students at elite schools and urban students balancing college with other demands: "My students have a hard time balancing the demands of their jobs, the demands of their families, and school. It's hard to know what to tell them, since I understand when they sometimes (or even often) have to priori-tize something other than my class." Adding an eloquent personal note, she writes:

> It's interesting coming from a place like Cornell, which was a totally different type of institution than where I am now (obviously). I so valued my time at Cornell and had always hoped to teach some place like it, but I find my work now so rewarding and important. These are students who need good teaching and someone who values them academically. So often that hasn't been the case for them.

(5) Come to every class on time, alert, prepared, and ready to take notes. In response to the above sentence, Peter Fortunato, Cornell '72, a former student of mine who taught as a lecturer at Ithaca College for years and at the Cornell Summer College, advises: "Learn how to take notes (most students, I've found, really don't know how to do this, or nowadays expect teachers to supply PowerPoint notes!) and how to connect writing and thinking, whatever the subject matter."

Work on your courses every day but not all day; do something that is fun and relaxing every day, whether it be formal activity like participation in an intramural sports or a singing group or a walk in the woods, a visit to a museum on or off campus, or a pick-up basketball game.

Fortunato observes: "Learn how to relax and focus, by taking either a stress-busting workshop or meditation class or guided relaxation class. Students do much better in college when they are intentional about these matters or have teachers who add such activities to class time."

Participating in Campus Life

(6) Experience complements what you learn in classes. Try to find summer jobs, campus jobs, and campus or community activities that parallel your goals. If you need or want a part-time job, try to get one compatible with your goals as a way to test whether you are on the right path. But also use jobs and activities to expand your horizons and interests.

Yet if financially possible, during term keep most of your time for academic work with some left over for extra-curricular activities and community volunteering.

In general if you are at an elite college or university, 10 or 12 hours on a paid job is enough. To be sure, at less demanding colleges and universities, many students – particularly older students, some of whom have families to support – carry a full course load and work a great many hours at jobs.

Gabrielle McIntire, Cornell Ph.D. '02 and a professor of English at Queen's University in Kingston, Ontario, Canada, advises:

> Prepare to work hard: this is the gateway and ticket to your whole future, and it is worth investing everything you have in this four-year period to keep those gates wide open so that you have as many choices as you possibly can upon graduation. I remember somehow figuring out as an undergrad that it was well worth my time to have a minimal part-time job (5 hours/week), and to use my "extra" time on pushing myself as hard as I could scholastically since that was the REAL investment in my future. That is, instead of earning $10/hour doing more part-time work, and thus having a bit more cash at hand in the moment, I realized that it would be better to be slightly poorer [as an] undergrad, which would then allow me to have many more rewards after [undergraduate years].

(7) Be sure to participate in one or more of the many campus activities, but during the first term choose a limited number until you are confident you can handle your course workload.

(8) Given that this is a tech-driven world, no matter what your major, develop tech skills, perhaps by taking basic courses in computer science if you have not already done so in high school. If you have done so, consider taking another one in college. Virtually every student who didn't develop tech skills has expressed regret to me.

Ryan Larkin, Cornell '14, advises: "Learning how to code (even basic HTML and CSS) would have been an invaluable step for me to take in high school, and some of the first advice I'd give to students would be to acquire hard technical skills that can add value to almost any kind of résumé."

Kyle Sullivan, Cornell '11, observes:

> [T]he world is developing at such a rapid pace and having the hard technical skills is almost a must in most job situations that aren't sales related. Although I'm in a sales position right now as a Small Business Commercial Lender for M&T Bank in New Jersey, I recently taught myself the basics of HTML, CSS, and Java through a website called codeacademy.com because that's something that won't change and will be quite valuable just for personal use moving forward.

Broadening Horizons and Expanding Interests

(9) Take advantage of lectures outside the areas of your coursework as well as special exhibits, campus theater presentations, musical and dance programs, and other campus resources, as well as the natural and/or urban treasures and cultural resources of the area in which your college is located.

(10) The world has become a Global Village. For you to be part of the village, you need to spend some time each day keeping informed about international and national news. That means reading a major newspaper in print or on the Internet like the *New York Times.*

Reflecting on conversations he had with fellow students, notably during the financial crises but also on other occasions, Kyle Sullivan notes:

> Some of my most valuable lessons in college came from the discourse I had with friends, friends from different upbringings and experiences that reflected their background and the places they came from or even visited for a brief or extended amount of time. Just having that intelligent and thoughtful discourse with them changed the way I look[ed] at a problem or a topic and changed the way I react[ed] to [it]. … I remember sitting in the fraternity house huddled around either CNN or MSNBC and switching to Fox News to get a different perspective and learning so much just from listening to the conversations being had from the other guys sitting around the TV.

Choosing Classes and Studying

(11) Think about your classes as communities of inquiry where you, your fellow students, and the professor are sharing intellectual curiosity, love of learning, and the desire to understand important subjects. I concur with what I have heard over the years:"If Prof. X [recognized at Cornell as a truly great professor] is teaching the Manhattan phone book, take it."

Rachel (Greengus) Schultz, Cornell '83, emphasizes:

> It is important to take interesting classes with great professors. Find out who the good teachers are and take their classes. Of course you need to be interested in the subject, but sometimes a great teacher can awaken a passion.
>
> I also think it is less about taking courses that fit your career path and more about taking classes that teach you how to think and learn. Success in adult life depends so much on being a life-long learner, and any tools you glean in college to hone this skill will set you up for success later in life.

Take classes that emphasize concepts and how to apply them. Learning by rote is much less important than learning how to think for yourself and to solve problems; the latter skills are crucial for your future. Be aware in your thinking of what you know, what you need to know, and what is unknowable.

But the right class for you may not be the right class for others. Emily Choi, Cornell '14, counsels: "I think it's always good to register for as many classes as you can, and to go in your first week, even if it's just to feel them out." If possible, when a class or professor is not fulfilling your expectations, drop the course.

Some students, especially in STEM subjects, enjoy study groups. As Zhongming Chen, Cornell '14 recalls:

> I felt that studying with friends was a key to my success. I … made a lot of close friends this way. It was a great way for me to bridge my major activities (academics, social life, and athletics) too. I understand that I may be a little biased though. I did head teams that created videos for the Learning Strategies Center that promoted these methods. I was that passionate about it! Also, this method may not be equally applicable to all majors (the videos my teams prepared were for the Biology and Chemistry Departments).

In small classes, participate in discussion and ask for clarification; in large ones, don't hesitate to ask questions if you have them and to visit the teaching assistant's or lecturer's office when you need help.

Peter Fortunato suggests: "Learn how you learn: that is, whether you are primarily an information-based (facts and figures), visual, auditory, 'hands-on,' or interpersonal (teamwork) based learner. Many professors and curricula assume that all students function in the same way in their respective courses."

Mark Eisner notes: "There is more to learning something than absorbing facts and techniques. Try to find opportunities to explain the subject matter to someone else, or to write an explanation in your own words. The best learning is active learning."

(12) Get to know at least one professor reasonably well each term. The professors who ask you about your plan of study, your goals, and your outside activities, and seem to care about you as a human being, will be not only resources whom you can go to for advice, but also potential future references. If one or more professors become your mentors – that is, mature, stable, thoughtful people for whom your personal and intellectual growth and future success in whatever you choose matter – you will be most fortunate. Although students are just as likely to find valuable mentors at large colleges as small ones, they may need to make more effort to reach out to and connect with professors. Even within the same college and university, department cultures are not the same. Where teaching is valued and teachers spend time with students, you are more likely to find a mentor.

Once you arrive at your school, I suggest visiting professors during office hours, showing interest in the subject (taking the initiative to do extra reading and then asking the professor about it), participating often and thoughtfully in class, as well as attending optional learning activities that the professor might offer. All of the aforementioned are ways to find a mentor at a college of any size.

For Becca Harrison, Cornell '14, finding a mentor was crucial:

> In high school, no one would have cared if I fell through the cracks; at Cornell (and probably many institutions), the minute I reached out to my chemistry professor and graduate student Freshman Writing Seminar instructor for help, I realized that finding a mentor who truly cared about my success made it possible to learn how to learn and work effectively.

Matt Barsamian, Cornell '04, advises:

> I think that [it] is invaluable [to get to know at least one professor well]. I was fortunate enough to get to know three or four professors/instructors fairly well. I would also emphasize the value of attending office hours and point out that they don't exist merely for those students who perceive themselves to be struggling to understand the material or in response to a bad grade on an exam or paper. I would highly recommend visiting every professor at least once during the semester during his/her office hours as an opportunity to connect. I think it also evidences a student's interest in and commitment to the course.

By knowing some of your professors, you will not only feel more a part of your college community, but you will also have necessary references for programs within college, work positions, and graduate school.

In "It Takes a Mentor," *New York Times* columnist Thomas L. Friedman has written:

> What are the things that happen at a college or technical school that, more than anything else, produce "engaged" employees on a fulfilling career track? According to Brandon Busteed, the executive director of Gallup's education division, two things stand out. Successful students had one or more teachers who were mentors and took a real interest in their aspirations, and they had an internship related to what they were learning in school.

(13) Find a few comfortable and quiet study places on campus, places where you work effectively and are not easily distracted. If you are commuting, you will still need to find places where you can focus on your academic work.

Maintaining Physical and Mental Health

(14) Participate in campus activities—teams, musical and dance groups, community activities that serve the underserved and aged— and take seminars that call upon collaborative action. Such collective endeavors give you an opportunity to develop group responsibilities, including social ethics and leadership skills necessary for later life. I am skeptical about the need for fraternities and sororities in 2014, a subject I will discuss later (Chapter 10, "The Greek System: Should You Join a Fraternity or Sorority?"), but they do respond to the social needs of many students.

Students who participate in campus activities get more out of their college experience and feel more satisfied with their college years both while at college and when looking back from a distance of years. Richard J. Light, in his book *Making the Most of College: Students Speak Their Minds*, notes that, based on surveys, "a substantial commitment to one or two activities other than coursework—for as much as twenty hours a week – has little or no relationship to grades. But such commitments *do* have a strong relationship to overall satisfaction with college life. More involvement is strongly correlated with higher satisfaction" (26).

(15) Remember the three Rs: Resilience (Falling down and getting up are one motion); Resourcefulness (Use your skills and intelligence, while drawing upon your experience); and Resolve (Pursue goals with determination and persistence). More likely than in high school, you are going to have disappointments and frustrations, but overcoming them is part of the process of preparing for the world beyond college.

In between completing her freshman year and beginning her sophomore year, Pauline Shongov, Cornell '17, observed: "[F]reshmen should never underestimate their talents but also should be humble in everything they do. If they strike a balance between these two, they will be open to everything college life has to offer and will thus win others' respect while maintaining self-respect in return."

(16) Look at setbacks and problems as challenges to be met and overcome; when you do so successfully, you will be gaining confidence to meet the next challenges. Learning to build on failures is an important quality for success, as many of my former students attest.

Becca Harrison, recalls "the value in *failing*, and not necessarily succeeding right out of the starting-gate that is freshman year." Recognize that all problems – personal and intellectual – are not neatly solved, and learn how to deal with complex and ambiguous questions.

Alyson Favilla, Cornell '16, adds:

> Adjusting personal expectations for success ... [and handling setbacks and problems require] significant perspective that isn't going to be available to students currently struggling with something that feels far out of their depth.

Many students, especially those from highly competitive, privileged areas, have never before had to confront the limitations of their own abilities. Recognizing those limits, and determining to improve on them, I think, is an important lesson; knowing that you can successfully apply yourself to difficult or new material is very different than expecting to understand it right away, or feeling disheartened when you do not. Similarly, success does not always engender satisfaction. Being good at something, or achieving conventional academic success at that thing, is not always a reason to pursue it. For me, that was an important thing to consider when deciding whether or not to switch programs.

(17) When you enter a new situation such as the first weeks at college, you might feel somewhat desperate to make friends quickly. But it is important to retain your core values and judgment and to avoid becoming part of a herd or doing things only because others are doing them.

Quoting *Psalm 139*, Cotton Mather advised his son going off to college: "[H]e that walketh with the Wise, shall be wise, but a companion of fools shall be destroyed. Shun the company of all profane and vicious persons, as you would the pestilence."

The period between entering school and Thanksgiving is sometimes known as the "Red Zone" because students are more prone to make bad choices, whether they partake excessively of substances that suspend their judgment or put up with physically abusive hazing or bullying roommates. It is no disgrace to change roommates or to move to a different floor or dorm. If you feel a situation is beginning to get out of control, do not be afraid to protest to campus authorities, or, if you feel the situation is dire, to call psychiatric services or the campus police.

Seek help when you need it, no matter what the issue. Mark Eisner, succinctly observes: "There is no shame in seeking help, and doing so can save your education and possibly even your life."

(18) Take care of yourself physically and emotionally. Be sure to get enough exercise and sleep, and be sure to eat regular nutritious meals. Sleep deprivation can lead to poor performance and poor judgment.

Mark Eisner puts it well:

> Sometimes you have to sacrifice what you could have learned through an all-nighter in order to get to bed at an hour that ensures a productive day the next day. Preferably you should set a regular bedtime and get to bed at that time each night. If there is not time to do everything, consider productivity in choosing which tasks to short change and when to sacrifice them. Studying course material (and thinking deeply about it) as you go along is more efficient than cramming at the end.

(19) Know that substance abuse is a problem on campuses, with alcohol being the most abused, and that use of alcohol and illegal drugs can lead to compromising situations in which judgment is skewed. Brad Berger, a father of a Dartmouth student and a reader of my *Huffington Post* articles, feels that colleges abnegate their responsibility in not enforcing laws that forbid underage drinking:

> When colleges allow drinking on the campuses, they are saying students and colleges can pick and choose what laws to break. Not only are they disregarding the drinking laws but also the behavior caused by the drinking is dangerous and destructive. Underage drinking in my opinion is the issue most important to colleges and least talked about.

(20) Laugh a lot and continue to develop your sense of humor. When things are not going well, remember you can't fix the past, but you can start where you are and create the future.

5

Nineteen Suggestions for College Sophomores

Introduction

As sophomores, students need to focus on planning for the future, something that should not be left to their senior year. Colleges and universities are becoming increasingly proactive about providing resources to help your planning. For example, the Cornell College of Arts and Sciences now has an Assistant Dean & Director of Career Services. What follows are 19 suggestions for sophomores who quite often are 19 years of age. I foreground my first three suggestions but after that there is no order.

(1) Sophomore year is a time to think about the future – whether it be employment or further education or a combination of both. With the future in mind, you should choose your college major, your summer employment and internships, your community service, and at least some of your extra-curricular activities. Think about preparing yourself for graduate school – medical, law, masters or Ph.D. – and find out what the requirements are. For example, many MBA programs prefer some years of work before graduate school.

Emily Choi, Cornell '14, observes:

> I think your emphasis on life after college here is really crucial. From my experience, I know a lot of the people I knew (myself included) really could have done a lot more [during their sophomore] year – not only in terms of taking the right classes or applying for the right internships, but staying in

How to Succeed in College and Beyond: The Art of Learning, First Edition. Daniel R. Schwarz.
© 2016 John Wiley & Sons, Ltd. Published 2016 by John Wiley & Sons, Ltd.

touch with our advisors and asking questions to the right people, whether it be our professors or our deans.

Develop your character in terms of self-knowledge, integrity, leadership, compassion, and judgment. Who you are becoming is as important as what skills you are developing.

(2) Think of your career plans or even your choice of major not in terms of future earnings but in terms of future satisfaction. Joy in work and joy in personal life are what give life meaning. Be aware, too, that the choice of major does not necessarily determine your future opportunities and that graduate schools and employees choose people with a range of skills, capabilities, and backgrounds, sometimes even deviating from standard qualifications in an effort to find the truly exceptional. According to Yoshika Toyoda, Cornell '14 and Weill Cornell Medical School '18:

> [G]rad schools take more interest and appreciate people with a broad perspective who may have double or triple majors. For medical school, you can major in anything as long as you take the core science classes. So many people I met at interviews were Psych or English or Spanish majors or double majors.

(3) If you are in the wrong program, think about changing it rather than investing even more time and energy in that program. If you are in the wrong college, think about transferring. After your sophomore year, such changes become more difficult.

(4) Be sure to choose an advisor who is interested in you and meet with your advisor regularly. Do not limit yourself to email communication. If your advisor doesn't keep his or her office hours, get another one. I recommend that if possible you choose an advisor who has been your teacher, because those who have taught you will know you better than an assigned advisor.

Many of the respondents to my *Huffington Post* articles have stressed the importance of finding a faculty member as an "academic mentor" who is, as Elliot Singer, Cornell '08, puts it, "not an 'advisor' in the traditional sense but someone who shares a mutual passion for an academic area" and shows the student intellectual and personal respect.

(5) If you have more than one passion, think about double majoring. The more skills you develop, the better for the job market and for the joy of learning.

(6) If possible, each term take at least one course far afield from your prospective major with the goal of expanding your interests. Try a basic course in creative writing or photography or acting. Remember that a course in music or art appreciation is an investment not only in your college experience, but in life. If you are an English major, take an economics course. If an engineer, take an English or history course. And so on.

(7) As a sophomore, you should, if at all possible, finish fulfilling all non-major requirements in order to be able to pursue your major and take other upper-level courses, including those in other fields.

(8) Make an effort to know your professors, in part to cultivate potential references, but also to take advantage of being around interesting minds. If a professor invites a class to go together to a theatrical or musical performance or to get together for a class dinner, don't miss that opportunity.

(9) Be sure you understand graduation requirements and major requirements; be aware that your advisor may not be conversant with all the requirements, and it is your responsibility to know them.

(10) Take classes from the best professors, who may also be the most demanding and not the easiest graders. Don't avoid classes that might jeopardize your GPA. Accept – indeed, pursue – challenges, for they are a source of intellectual growth. If you are taking classes that are far from your expertise and skills, you can at most colleges take these classes without any grade other than pass/fail or satisfactory/unsatisfactory. In my experience, students who take courses in fields different from their majors do fine and grow. In fact, overcautiously protecting one's GPA can be a strategy that limits growth and fulfillment of potential and can affect your future willingness to think boldly and imaginatively.

(11) Look for professors who are interested in students as people and want to know about your progress in college and your future plans.

(12) As much as possible, balance smaller classes with larger ones. Realize that sometimes you learn more from a professor who knows his or her field and mostly lectures than you learn in a discussion-size class where a half-prepared professor begins each class session with, "What do we all think about this?"

(13) Stay physically fit; if you are not fit, make that a high priority by choosing some physically demanding activities like running or swimming or going to a campus gym regularly or joining a private gym. Choose your friends wisely, and avoid those who overindulge in alcohol and rely on illegal substances. Be very careful whom and what you text and what you put on social media because these messages can come back to haunt you.

Learn from your fellow students; spend time with students who are committed to the act of learning. Informal communities of inquiry will supplement your formal course instruction.

(14) Use the campus cultural resources: theater, music, arts, and museums. Yoshika Toyoda advises: "Throughout all [your college] years, take advantage of what is unique to your college. Enjoy the recreational activities, classes, arts, that are specific to your university! Explore quads and buildings you never went to before you leave!" It can be great fun to walk into buildings you have never visited and take an evening to study there. You may not only find a new favorite study spot and/or campus café, but possibly make new friends.

(15) Participate in activities on campus: debating, religious groups, college newspaper, sports – for most students, this will mean intramural or club sports rather than varsity – musical and acting groups, etc. Also be a part of the larger community as a volunteer by tutoring underserved communities, helping the elderly, reading to the blind, or teaching at a local prison.

Emily Choi recalls: "While it's important to stay focused, I myself benefited from trying at least one new thing each semester. While these new activities might not grow into strengths, I think it helped relax me, giving me something productive to do during what otherwise would have been filled with naps or Netflix."

(16) Develop leadership skills in organizations; belong to groups in which your initiative matters. Usually extra-curricular group leaders – such as editors from the school newspaper, captains of athletic teams, or officers of campus organizations – come from participants who begin these activities in their freshman and sophomore years.

Helen Maxson, retired Professor of English, Southwestern Oklahoma State University, wisely adds: "[Students] sometimes feel that their influence on things beyond themselves is negligible. Contributing to a group's activities is a good way for them to learn to take themselves more seriously. The confidence sneaks up on them. They start to be aware of it and slowly come to trust it."

(17) Think about whether studying abroad as a junior is for you. The first term of your sophomore year is the best time to plan for this. Application dates vary from program to program. For a full junior year or fall term abroad, you often need to apply in the fall of your sophomore year. For the spring term abroad as a junior, you can wait until the second term of your sophomore year to apply for some programs. I believe that study abroad for a term or a year is a terrific experience because you will live in another culture and learn new perspectives.

(18) No matter what your major, take courses that emphasize communication skills, notably expository writing and speaking. Whatever you do, you will need to be articulate and write precise, clear, coherent, and well-organized prose. Take advantage of public speaking opportunities.

(19) Finally, time is your most precious commodity. Use your time effectively and keep track of how you are using it.

6

Suggestions for College Juniors: Balancing the Joy and Practicality of Learning

Introduction

The problem for today's college students, and especially juniors, is how to balance the practicality of learning – career and grad school preparation – with the joy of learning. I think of junior year as a bridge between the college experience and the post-graduate experience. It is your next-to-last year in the college incubator, but one that looks forward to a time when the college experience is over.

It is a year for testing and refining values, for discovering who you are and who you want to be. Obviously this is a process begun in grade school – and, hopefully, continuing throughout your life – but it comes to a head in the later college years. Key words in junior year are "proactive," "imaginative," "experimental," as well as, on the practical side, "dossier building" (which means that summer internships and work experience before and after your junior year are important). Even as you zero in on career and graduate student goals, you should make an effort to hone your communication and listening skills.

Junior year is the time to separate the wheat from the chaff in terms of making lifetime friends as opposed to superficial partying and to emphasize health and fitness. If excessive and binge drinking has been an issue, it is time for moderation and self-control.

Junior year is the time to broaden your horizons, reach out beyond your immediate circles, and develop your skills at seeing the points of view of others. Certainly developing tolerance is a goal that encompasses the joy and practicality of learning. If your generation learns to communicate ideas in civil nuanced discourse,

How to Succeed in College and Beyond: The Art of Learning, First Edition. Daniel R. Schwarz.
© 2016 John Wiley & Sons, Ltd. Published 2016 by John Wiley & Sons, Ltd.

logically and lucidly – presented in such a way that there is space for discussion and rejoinders – all of us will have the pleasure of living in a less polarized and more civil society where democracy functions and diverse perspectives are respected.

(1) If at all possible, take a junior term or year abroad and participate in the Global Village. Having studied abroad my junior year, I am a strong proponent of that experience and urge everyone who can to take advantage of the opportunity. After 53 years I still think that spending a year in Edinburgh while attending Edinburgh University was a transformative year in my life. Without email and with phone calls being very expensive for my frugal parents, I was really on my own, much more so than at a residential college in the US. I travelled all over Western and Central Europe and even took a month-long train trip – rare for its day – into Eastern Europe, mostly Russia but with some days in Poland.

Going abroad often makes young adults better citizens by offering them a more cosmopolitan perspective on how the world works than they can get at home. Some of this comes from meeting students from other countries. Even students from other countries who are fellow guests may be more open to you as a US citizen than when in the US.

By encountering new challenges, you will learn more about yourself. Students usually return with greater self-confidence, poise, and maturity. Keep a journal of your experiences and think about the consequences of your experiences. Nothing teaches you how to think better and at a higher level than new experiences and new situations.

As an English major, I was restricted to British universities, and Oxford and Cambridge in 1961–2 did not welcome American Juniors, but today's students have a wide array of universities to choose from. They now take a term or a year not only in Britain and France, but also in such places as Sydney, Seville, Cape Town, Prague, and Buenos Aires, to say nothing of Kathmandu, Nepal and Dakar, Senegal.

Even though the world is much more connected electronically than when I did my junior year in Scotland, and my parents and I communicated entirely by snail mail (except for their one three-day visit), students still will need to rely more on their own resources when in a new environment and also need to make new friends.

I have very rarely heard a student returning to her or his home university with regret about taking a term or year abroad. The experience of studying in a different country and in many cases in a foreign language enables you to live in a different culture and among a diverse group of students unlike those in your American university. While many US colleges and universities now have an international inflexion with more and more foreign students coming here to study, the normative values – educational and otherwise – reflect those of the United States; foreign guests tend to adapt to the dominant US culture. But when you are the foreign guest in another country, the values of that country's culture dominate and you need to adjust.

Virtually every country in the world has a concept of its own exceptionalism, something we assume is ours alone. People take pride in their own history and culture even if they come from countries that some politicians and even news media in the US patronize as "Third World" and are therefore regarded as insignificant in the world's geopolitics or discounted as being in social and political disarray. But keeping up with the international news regularly– notably in the *New York Times* or the *Economist* – will enable you to understand the multi-faceted reality within countries. For example, one might think of Nigeria as a place where a radical Islamic group called Boko Haram kidnaps young girls. But Nigeria is also the most populous country in Africa with the largest economy and with an impressive history and culture.

During your term or year abroad, you may not work as hard or learn as much in terms of coursework as at your home university. But learning takes place outside the classroom as you are exposed to different political systems and different social customs. Living in a different culture outside the comfort zone that you have developed in your first few years of college, your learning will take new forms. You will not only be reading history, you will – as you immerse yourself in another culture – be experiencing history.

Your assumptions about how the world is organized politically and socially will be challenged. You will discover that many of the truths that you were taught and take for granted will be questioned. You may think that the US is the land of opportunity as well as the protector and paradigm of economic and political freedom, but others may see the US differently.

Learning about other cultures and languages is best done, in my judgment, through travel. Students from other countries need to visit the US and we need to visit other countries. Travelling is education from life experience and complements education from books and professors. While abroad, you should travel as much as possible. The opportunity to complement the experience of studying at another university with travel within and beyond the country where you are studying is another major benefit of a junior year abroad. Be sure to visit as many countries as you can and to see as much of your host country as you can. My junior year abroad turned me into a lifetime traveller.

If you study in Europe, you will be much more conscious of Hitler's rise and fall, of the effects of the Second World War, and of the Holocaust. If you study in Eastern Europe, you will discover that the military presence of the USSR from 1945 to 1989 and the effects of the Communist experiment inform every day of life in 2015. In the Balkans, you experience firsthand the costs of the terrible wars that divided the old Yugoslavia. In Russia or China, you will not only be living under different social and economic assumptions, but will also be exposed to far different views of the United States.

A personal note: In 1962, while driving across Germany in an inexpensive car that I bought, I stopped at a bed and breakfast. I came downstairs the next morning to see pictures of an SS officer on the wall. In Rome, a Jewish woman with a number tattooed on her wrist approached me in the street because she correctly took me to be an American Jew. One night I wandered around Moscow with a friend because the subways had stopped running and we were miles from our hotel. In St. Petersburg, we met a young woman who was the granddaughter of a nuclear physicist and who wanted us to help her leave Russia; we went to the American Embassy on her behalf and were told something might be possible were the physicist the person who wanted to leave and that we were in all probability being followed by the KGB. These experiences taught me a great deal about post-war Europe.

If you are not studying abroad in an English-speaking country, you will develop language facility. While some assume that English is the lingua franca of the world, learning foreign languages is more important than ever. Yes, many US campuses have international students, but people who are guests may be more inhibited about expressing their views and in some cases they may have not as good a command of English as they do of their native language. If you understand the language spoken in their own country, you may be exposed to a wide variety of views and perhaps more nuanced ones.

While it is difficult to study abroad in some fields – particularly engineering – because of the large set of required courses in a tight four-year sequence, more and more departments and colleges are encouraging students to try to find a way to do so. For example, the Cornell College of Engineering manages three exchange programs: Universidad de Cantabria in Spain, Hong Kong University of Science and Technology, and Technion–Israel Institute of Technology. Yet at this point at most colleges, only a small fraction of engineering students go abroad.

Alex Kwonji Rosenberg, Cornell '10, observes that working abroad can be an alternative to studying abroad:

> There are other opportunities out there if students don't want to give up a semester in school or prefer not to take classes even if they want to experience life abroad. I didn't participate in a study abroad program per se, but I did work for Foundation for Sustainable Development in Uganda during the summer of my sophomore year. A classmate also conducted research with the ICTY [International Criminal Trubunal for the Former Yugoslavia] under the Frederic Conger Wood Fellowship. I would argue these opportunities are even more meaningful depending on what your goals are. I think it's extremely important to test your boundaries but also to serve others. Working abroad can offer that. It can also be a way to merge classroom learning with experiential learning.

Practical Advice on Junior Year Abroad

Do not spend too much of your time with students from your own US college if they are in the same program. Take courses with host country professors rather than with American professors who are sent along with students in some programs. Usually it is best to enroll directly in the host university rather than be part of a satellite program provided by an American university. If possible, live with foreign students not fellow Americans and certainly not with close friends from your own college.

If you are planning an entire year abroad, you need to choose courses in your sophomore year that put you on track to fulfill a major and, in some cases, do an honors program. If you need to take honors seminars before writing an honors essay, be sure to do so before your junior year abroad.

Even if you are only going abroad for one term, you will still need to be attentive to what courses you need to take and which will count toward your degree and major from your courses abroad. The key when going abroad is to be sure that all your requirements for graduation and major are covered and that your major advisor and the major department's Director of Undergraduate Study and/or whoever needs to sign off on your plans are consulted and in the loop so as to avoid any misunderstanding about credits and requirements for the major upon your return.

(2) Offered by more than 50 colleges, the best alternative to a term or year abroad may be a term in Washington, especially for a Government or American History major. David Silbey, Cornell '90, Director of Cornell's Washington program, observes:

> I think the value of the Cornell in Washington program comes from its combination of academic and practical challenges. By marrying intensive classwork with the on-the-ground experience of working in DC, students gain an understanding of the political and policy world in a way not possible in Ithaca.

Cornell's semester in Washington program includes an internship where you will get practical experience.

Off-campus study opportunities will vary from college to college but they continue to increase. Another possibility at some colleges is a term in New York, especially for those focused on the arts. For example, Cornell's College of Architecture, Art, and Planning offers both an optional (usually) sophomore term in New York City and an optional junior year term in Rome, and many Cornell students in that college do both.

Changing your venue and your immediate associates will open doors and windows to new ways of thinking and new experiences. Many colleges, including Cornell's College of Engineering, have junior year co-op programs in which students may spend a term in industry, preceded by an extra summer of coursework when they take the courses that they would have taken in the first semester of their junior year. At Cornell, co-op programs are also open to College of Arts and Sciences sophomores in Computer Science, and College of Agriculture and Life Sciences sophomores in Biological and Environmental Engineering.

(3) The junior year is a time for engagement in a specific field of study, otherwise known as a major, and that concentration of courses in a particular area can bring not only depth to your learning but also the satisfaction of knowing that you have the tools and information to solve problems and to confront issues with competence. If you are in a STEM program – STEM is an acronym referring to the academic disciplines of science, technology, engineering, and mathematics – your curriculum will have more required courses in sequence and thus be more tightly organized. You will be taking courses in your major that build on proficiency attained in more basic courses. If you are in the sciences, you will be developing necessary skills for a job after graduation or for graduate school. In most of the aforementioned fields, you should explore the possibility of doing research under the umbrella of professors' labs and research grants. For one thing, honing in on individual research projects will enable you to see if a research career is for you.

At Cornell's Engineering College, Mark Eisner, Cornell Ph.D. '70, writes, "[T]here is an active program to engage the students in research. ... Really strong undergraduates do get their names on published papers from time to time. ... [U]ndergraduate project teams ... are particularly popular and valuable in engineering." Professor David Delchamps, Cornell Associate Professor of Electrical and Computer Engineering, adds: "Many engineering undergraduates participate in research. Sometimes they do it for pay (which often comes from external research grants and contracts), but usually they do it for academic credit."

As I am stressing throughout, the more important skills that you will acquire should be to think critically, write lucidly and precisely, and know how to marshal evidence to make an argument, and express yourself articulately without a plethora of "umm"s and "you know"s.

If you have trouble expressing yourself in class or simply want to improve your speaking skills, junior year is an excellent time for a public speaking course, providing your school has such courses. Another place to develop verbal facility is the debating club, albeit the earlier that one begins that activity – even in high school – the better.

Mark Eisner observes:

> It may be easier to teach humanities graduates how to use a spreadsheet, prepare a specification, and build a financial case than to teach STEM graduates how to write, speak, read, reason, understand, relate, and create. Of course these humanities graduates need to be open to applying their intellect to mastering such mundane tasks, rather than falling back on "I'm not good at math" and running away from them.

(4) Balancing the practicality of learning with the joy of learning, the junior year is also a time to explore campus resources. You should strive to develop a few new interests, whether they be taking a creative writing course, writing for the school newspaper for the first time, learning about classical music, practicing yoga, auditioning for parts in plays, taking up a new musical instrument, or learning how to cook.

(5) Choosing a minor in either a parallel or unrelated field to your major can be broadening. The minor is fairly new at Cornell and it enables upperclassmen to branch out and complement their practical major with forays into the humanities, and vice versa.

(6) If you have an opportunity to do an honors thesis, and thus do independent research, I advise taking it. To work on and complete an independent project is a wonderful experience in building self-confidence and developing intellectual curiosity and love of learning as well as a way to polish your CV for the job market or for your graduate school application.

(7) As you prepare for the future, junior year is a time for growth and maturation. This can take many forms, including expanding your competence and experience, both intellectually and personally. Even partial mastery of complex academic fields and completion of relatively sophisticated projects builds self-confidence to pursue even more difficult projects. If possible, it is a time to test and develop your leadership skills in one of the extra–curricular activities in which you are involved.

Sylvia Rusnak, Cornell '15, recalls:

> As a senior now, I would most certainly agree that my junior year was a key year, balancing both joy and practicality of learning. I started to learn more about yoga last year, I became involved in my psychology research lab (in which I am now working on an honors thesis), and I signed up to complete the French minor. I also had a wonderful internship this past summer. I was interning with the domestic research & evaluation department at Sesame Workshop (aka Sesame Street).

Lucy Goss, Cornell '14, who did the second term of her junior year in Sydney after her first term at Cornell, comments:

> One thing I would add about [my] junior year … was becoming comfortable with being alone. Whether it be going to a new country by yourself with study abroad or simply beginning to spend more time on campus alone, I find junior year to be a time to become more comfortable with your own company and not having to go everywhere with a group of friends. It allows you to learn more about what interests you personally and maybe even make new and different friends [whom] you didn't think [in your] freshman and sophomore years [would now be your friends].

Lucy's comment about learning to be alone and growing from that experience of relying on one's own resources mirrors my experience in 1961–2 when I was abroad for both terms.

(8) What you do in the summers between your sophomore and junior years and between your junior and senior years is important. Look for internships that might expose you to job opportunities or build references and experience for graduate school placement. In media fields – newspapers, magazine journalism, television, Internet companies – this seems particularly important for getting post-graduate employment. But building networks to help with placement after graduation – whether in employment or graduate school – matters in every field.

(9) In looking for jobs on campus during your junior year, think about the future. Thus if you are interested in publishing, positions with a university press, the university publication office, or the alumni magazine will help. If you are a STEM student and can find a paying job, working in labs and on technology projects would be a good idea.

Yoshiko Toyoda, Cornell '14, adds:

> It is also somewhat difficult to find a paid job as a researcher. However, many of my friends took advantage of merit scholarships and research fellowship opportunities available for juniors. These ranged from national scholarships such as the Goldwater or Truman to university-specific scholarships such as the Bio-Res/Rawlings Presidential Research Scholar award. It would be wise of the students to stay in constant contact with the scholarship office throughout their four years for such opportunities!

(10) Choose some extra-curricular activities with the future in mind, but choose at least one because it expands your interests. The debating club would be a good activity for law school or a career in politics, the student newspaper for a career in journalism, and so forth. If you want to be a professional

64

musician, you should obviously try out for the college band or orchestra or the jazz ensemble. If you wish to perform in music or dance or stand-up comedy, you can develop those skills by performing while in college.

As a junior, you should try to develop at least one new activity that is fun and has lifetime potential, whether it be athletic, such as biking, tennis, or golf, or cultural, such as joining a drama group or developing an interest in African art.

(11) If graduate school in medicine, law, STEM advanced studies, or humanities (either Ph.D. or MA) is in your plans, you must think about such admission tests as MCAT (medical school), LSAT (law school), GRE (post-graduate Ph.D. or MA), GMAT (Graduate Management programs), or DAT (Dental). Many students take preparation courses for these exams, and others choose to study for themselves.

Doing well on these exams is a component of successful application. Paradoxically, with grade inflation – and this means grade conflation where so many students have similarly high grades – these exams tend to count more in the admission process than they once did. One argument made by graduate schools for using standard tests is that test scores enable them to distinguish between students having comparable GPAs at different colleges. Thus if one student has a 3.9 GPA from Dartmouth and another one gets the same from a less competitive college, the test enables a graduate school program to see if they are equally qualified or not.

This reliance on standard tests is especially true of law school admission, where I find that, based on LSAT numbers, I can predict with some exactness which schools will admit a student. Medical schools still have an interviewing process, but most other graduate programs do not.

(12) Juniors need to be thinking about potential future references. They should get to know some of their professors in smaller classes or, if they are only taking larger ones, cultivate a relationship with their major advisor and at least one professor. But references can also come from faculty supervising research or from those supervising summer employment that is relevant to their post-graduate career or graduate school program.

Yoshiko Toyoda counsels: "Even if students are only in large classes, there are many opportunities to get to know the professor! Go to their office hours or set up appointments, ask them questions after lectures, etc. If you are persistent enough, they will remember you!"

Conclusion

Junior year is the time to both narrow your focus on what you plan on doing and expand your focus in terms of interests, skills, and who you are and want to be. Test yourself and enjoy the process.

7

Making the Most of Your Senior Year in College

Introduction

Your senior year is a time when you must balance academic work with seeking employment or applying for graduate school, and when the clock is running out on your precious undergraduate years. Your senior year rounds out a four-year – sometimes longer, especially for part-time students – investment of time and life experience, and you want to bring it to as fulfilling a conclusion as possible. You may have entered college as an 18-year-old adolescent, but your goal should be to leave as an adult ready to confront the challenging world of graduate school or employment.

You need to balance the joy and the practicality of learning. Key concepts are "preparation," "innovation," "experimentation," and "motivation." I shall divide my suggestions between "making the most of your campus experience" and "preparation for the future."

Making the Most of Your Campus Experience

What Anne Kenney, Head of Cornell's Library System, counsels is especially true for your senior year: "I think having proper balance, being open to wonder and curiosity as well as [doing your] academic work, is so key."

(1) Repeating what I wrote in my advice to juniors: If you have a chance to write an honors thesis and/or to do individual supervised

How to Succeed in College and Beyond: The Art of Learning, First Edition. Daniel R. Schwarz.
© 2016 John Wiley & Sons, Ltd. Published 2016 by John Wiley & Sons, Ltd.

research or independent study, take advantage of those opportunities. Working closely with a top professor who takes an interest in your work can be an exciting learning experience. Emily Choi, Cornell '14, emphasizes: "One of the most valuable skills I take away from my senior year is the ability to revise. It's so important to be able to look at your work candidly, and to evaluate it, and find creative solutions for the parts that could change for the better." In the first term of her senior thesis work in psychology, Sylvia Rusnak, Cornell '15, observed: "My honors thesis thus far has proved to be an important learning experience. Of course it's stressful and immensely time-consuming and frustrating at (many) times, but to have the responsibility to run my own research study in a lab is an opportunity I feel so grateful to have."

The process of doing independent research or writing an honors thesis may help you decide whether you have the skills and passion to pursue a Ph.D. and a research career. To do so, you need to enjoy thinking about your project every day. In my experience, those who succeed as research scholars are virtually fixated on their projects over a long period of time. Before one project is completed, they already have the next foregrounded in their minds.

(2) Presumably by now you have fulfilled your requirements. Senior year is a good time to take elective courses in new areas, perhaps even to try a different foreign language, which might also help make you attractive to employers with an international business component. (Of course, beginning languages earlier, perhaps in high school, can be a better way to develop proficiency.)

Senior year is also a good time to take courses that develop your under-standing of music, art, architecture, and literature, that is, to invest in lifetime activities. If you are majoring in a liberal arts field such as history or philosophy, you might consider a course in government (called political science, at some schools) or economics. If you are concerned about grades, you can take these classes at most colleges on a pass/fail or satisfactory/unsatisfactory basis.

As a senior, try something new in terms of extra-curricular activities, whether it is a new sport, acting in plays, photography, painting, or some other endeavor.

(3) While one cannot compartmentalize emotional problems, senior year is a good time to solve personal issues within the somewhat protective world of college, and those issues include substance abuse issues like binge or excessive drinking.

(4) Go beyond the comfort zone that you have established in your earlier years. Make a conscious effort to make new friends and spend time with people who are not your closest associates. If you are in a fraternity or sorority, reach beyond those enclaves. Benefit from the ethnic and class diversity at your college. Learn, too, the value of alone time when you depend on your own resources and when you can respond independently and thoughtfully to the world around you and your experiences.

(5) Think of your senior year as another stage in personal growth and becoming the person you want to be. Continue to develop your potential as a leader as well as your ability to work on projects as a team. Within a group context, explaining an idea or concept to a fellow student can help you understand it better.

Most campus organizations have leadership opportunities for seniors. Leading sometimes means helping to create a cooperative environment or community where everyone participates, has input, and feels part of projects. Obviously a penchant for leadership emerges before your senior year, and leadership qualities begin developing in high school and even junior high school

University of South Carolina Professor of English and Comparative Literature Scott Gwara advises:

> In your campus focus groups (friends, partners, colleagues with common inter-ests) discover what your leadership passion is. ... In discovering your leadership, harnessing your network, and finding campus/personal/spiritual resources, you should articulate a vision of yourself and your interactions with the environment you want to change. ... Connect to the facts but make your vision big enough to inspire. Set an agenda. Decide to make a difference and *persist*. You will learn about your limitations, your ethics, and your leadership capacities. By the time you graduate, you will have accomplished something meaningful, even if your primary accomplishment is learning not to take *no* for an answer. By all means, learn the art of pushing back.

Certainly, learning how to negotiate with those resistant to your ideas is an important skill, blending preparation (knowing the facts), enthusiasm, poise, and courtesy with the ability to organize and articulate an argument. Indeed, many of these qualities can be developed within small classes, especially seminars. But all the aforementioned qualities are part of becoming an effective adult, ready to play a part in the larger world of work and civic responsibility.

One of my pleasures as a teacher is observing the process by which bright adolescents on the threshold of adulthood become confident adults, ready to play an important role in their chosen profession and society, although of course the process continues in their twenties and should continue throughout their lives.

(6) Spend some time each day learning about the world beyond your campus. Reading the *New York Times* online or in print is one good way to fulfill my recommendation that you give a half hour a day to learning outside your courses about fields you know little about. For liberal arts students, the

New York Times Science Times section, which appears on a Tuesday, is a good learning opportunity. I also recommend the *New York Review of Books*; much more than a collection of book reviews, it is, along with the *Economist*, an essential publication for understanding the world.

(7) Seniors interviewing for employment positions need to be aware that the employment world does not operate on the academic calendar or clock. Liberal arts students accustomed to awaking at 10 and going to bed in the wee hours of the morning need to learn that much of the world awakens at 7 or before and also that Thursday – the day many liberal arts students end their class week – does not end the work week in the employment world. Nor is there time in the work world to compensate with an afternoon nap for sleeping only three hours. A humorous personal example: some months after my older son's graduation from college, where his bedtime was in the 3 a.m. range, I remember calling him at 11:05 p.m.; then employed in NYC's financial world, he growled: "Don't you know we go to bed at night and get up in the morning here?"

Preparation for the Future: Looking Beyond Your Undergraduate Experience

(1) You need to be sure you know the qualifications for the career and graduate programs you have chosen. While pre-law and pre-med programs often make this clear, it may take some research to know how to prepare for careers in teaching, journalism, pharmacy, nursing, actuarial science, etc.

(2) You need to continue to develop skills of time management. I recommend, as I have in previous chapters, keeping a log on how you are spending your time. In your senior year, unless you are taking a gap year, you will be balancing your coursework not only with extra-curricular activities and perhaps a job, but also with making time for job interviews and applications for graduate school. If you are looking for employment or interviewing for medical schools or non-profits such as Teach for America, you may find yourself taking several trips away from campus.

Studying for the LSAT, MCAT, and GRE exams is time consuming. In fact, as I mentioned in my advice to juniors, the summer between your junior and senior years may be the best time to study for these tests. You usually take these tests in the calendar year prior to the year you will be applying for entrance. Thus if you seek entrance in 2016, you would take the exam in 2015, but early enough to have the LSAT scores when you decide what schools to apply to. If you don't do as well as you wish, you may take these tests again.

Matt Barsamian, Cornell '04, observes:

> The LSAT is, unfortunately, a very important piece of the law school admissions regime, and seniors should consider whether they can truly prepare for the LSAT well enough to get a very strong score while also maintaining excellent grades in their courses – for many, I think doing so would mean sacrificing one or the other or both (I can't imagine preparing for the LSAT while writing my honors thesis).

The MCAT exam is often taken in the second half of the junior year, and it is given in January, March, April, and May, but some students prefer to take it in the summer. On the whole I recommend taking the LSAT in June after your junior year, but if you wish more time to study, the early fall test might work better. Most medical and law schools have rolling admission, which means they begin to accept students and fill classes as the applications arrive. (While what medical schools look for varies from school to school, Ibrahim Busnaina's article "Avoid 4 Medical School Admission Myths" may be helpful).

(3) You need to learn about your campus Career Service and Placement offices and resources. Not only will these offices have organized schedules of which employers are visiting campuses to interview candidates – often taking the form of Job Fairs – but also they will have tips for interviewing and preparing CVs as well as for writing both appropriate cover letters and personal statements. You need to set up a file at these Career Service and Placement offices. In addition to helping students find employment, these offices can be helpful with applying to graduate school, although some schools also have special offices and committees for law school and medical school applications.

Professors who have shown an interest in you can also be important resources. Not only can they advise you on the best plans for entering certain fields, but they also might be able to put you in touch with influential people they know, including former students, who may be hiring.

(4) Learn how to interview; this means learning not only how to speak but also how to dress appropriately, guidelines for which vary depending on the organization and even on the person with whom you are interviewing. Teach For America has different expectations for presentable dress than investment banking. My younger son has made it very clear to me that dress within the mutual fund industry is more oriented to suit and tie for men and comparable attire for women than our dress expectations in the academic world.

(5) Think about whether a gap year is right for you. If you are undecided about your future career or you want more time to prepare for the GRE exams,

MCAT, or LSAT, or you feel you need a rest from the demands of study, taking a year between undergraduate and graduate school can be a good idea. It may be advisable in STEM fields to limit the gap to a year because you might forget some of what you have learned.

Taking time between college and graduate school sometimes provides a necessary space for different kinds of learning and experiences. Some students work on a political campaign, others take a few years to teach in other countries or join the Peace Corps. But there are a huge number of worthwhile possibilities. Schools offering an MBA want their applicants to have a handful of years of work experience.

Conclusion

Your senior year in college is an excellent opportunity to bring your undergraduate years to fruition and to open doors to the next phases of your growth and development.

8

Planning for the Future: Suggestions for Seniors Graduating from College

I am going to divide my suggestions for how to plan the future into two categories – "future plans" and "life after college" – although, of course, they overlap.

Future Plans

(1) The time to begin thinking about what you will be doing after graduation – whether it be graduate school, law school, medical school, dental school, or entering the work world – is well before graduation, that is, when you are you are a freshman or perhaps a sophomore. For graduate programs, you need to know what the requirements are. To be sure, you may change direction. But choosing your courses, major, on- and off-campus activities, summer work (including internships), and even whether and where to study abroad during your junior year are all part of this process. This does not mean everything you do must be directed to your future plans, but it does mean you should not be an ostrich – burying your head in the sand – about the future.

For some, as noted before, a gap year between college and graduate school is often a good idea. The gap year (or two) can be a time to polish your credentials with activities such as doing research before applying to medical school or studying for LSATs, if you think that will give a better chance to get the score necessary for the level of schools to which you wish to apply. It can mean working in a law office to see if law is a field that suits you

How to Succeed in College and Beyond: The Art of Learning, First Edition. Daniel R. Schwarz.
© 2016 John Wiley & Sons, Ltd. Published 2016 by John Wiley & Sons, Ltd.

(although be aware that you may be getting a frog's perspective because your view is from the lower echelons).

Matt Barsamian, Cornell '04, advises:

> I would recommend taking a year or two to take stock and make sure that law is really what one wants to do – or that a law degree is really the ideal vehicle for doing the kinds of work one is interested in doing. Talking to law students and lawyers is helpful, and working in a law firm or at least around lawyers could be very useful for getting an understanding of what they do day in and day out.

If you are thinking of a Ph. D. program, a gap year may give you a chance not only to study for the GRE exam, including the subject test, but also to compete with those who have already graduated and perhaps received honors and been elected to Phi Beta Kappa. When you apply during your senior year, your credentials may be less polished than they will be the next year. The gap year is a chance to catch your breath and perhaps an opportunity to live and work in a place where you have always wanted to reside. A gap year or two can also give you a chance to earn some money, particularly if you are in a field with decent starting salaries like engineering.

(2) Your first choice for employment should usually be a position where the employer is thinking about where you will be in a few years, rather than how much money you will make in the short term for the company. Usually, the best positions are those in which you have a chance to learn and grow and not those where you are used simply to sell something without getting much training. In the latter case, you are an interchangeable cog and are probably not in the employer's long-range plans. When you are offered a position, learn as much as you can about the culture of the employer, including whether employees stay, advance, and are well-treated.

(3) Summer internships – whether paid or not – are a way to get to know an organization and for the organization to get to know you. Thus internships are often a bridge to employment with the organization.

Matt Barsamian notes:

> I think internships and summer jobs are very useful. Of course it is always good to get substantive experience in the field you intend to work in, but just as useful, in my estimation, is simply getting the experience of being comfortable in a professional setting – being in an office, arriving on time, dressing professionally … attending meetings … and generally interacting the way people do in an office. I think there is a value to showing up on the first day of work somewhere and being able to act like you belong there.

A publicist and artist manager in the music industry, Colin Ilgen, Cornell '04, advises:

> As far as gaining practical experience, generally in the music industry companies will not hire recent graduates unless they intern and gain work experience in the later half of their college career. It doesn't matter if you graduate from a top-tier school. If you don't pay your dues as an intern, it makes it incredibly difficult to gain entry into the field.

(4) Cast your eye widely when applying for positions. Sometimes organizations will find applicants who don't quite fit their posted job specifications more interesting than those who are more obvious candidates and thus will invite such applicants for interviews.

(5) In a first interview – and indeed through the hiring process if you are just out of college – the prospective employer is mostly in charge, but once you are offered a position, you can be pro-active in asking questions and perhaps contacting other employees. Of course, later on, when you have acquired skills and stature and you are shopping for a new position while holding a good one, you can be more aggressive in the early stages of the hiring process.

(6) Learn as much as possible about the company interviewing you. Prepare for interviews in advance by anticipating questions. It is a good idea to write down questions and answers so that you are not responding with "you know" and "umm." Recording your answers so you can listen to yourself is a good idea. Practicing with a friend is also helpful.

Yoshiko Toyoda, Cornell '14, advises:

> For interview questions, there are … many useful [online sources] for possible interview questions. For medical students, there is the "Student Doctor Network" online, where past interviewees list all of the questions they were asked. In addition, there was [at Cornell] a student advising service through which you can schedule mock interviews with trained staff. I went to several of these and my other classmates utilized these very frequently and found them helpful.

(7) Interviews are the chance to show why you are the person for the position, and you need to make sure by the end of an interview that you have given the interviewer the information that makes you special. If the company is hiring four people, finishing fifth is not good enough.

(8) The kindergarten criterion "Works well with others" is at least as important after graduation as before. Organizations and businesses put more and more emphasis on hiring people who have experience working on group projects and interacting effectively on a sustained basis with other employees. In interviews and even in your letter of application, it is a good idea to stress how you have done cooperative group work in the past, either in internships or academic work, and to give specific examples.

(9) Self-presentation in terms of speaking well, showing your initiative, convincing an employer or a selection board that you have much to offer, and, yes, having an appropriate appearance are all important in interviews. In fact, self-presentation is also important on a day-to-day basis and you will be judged on it.

(10) Respect diversity in the workplace, and seek diversity among friends.

(11) Once you take a position or enroll in a graduate program, you have chosen a path. Give your choice your full effort and give yourself every chance to succeed by making a full commitment. There will be plenty of time to change direction, and it is fine to do so if you decide after giving a situation a real chance that you have made the wrong choice.

Be aware that staying the course is considered by many a virtue, and flitting from one path to another every six months is not an advertisement for your persistence or stability when applying to graduate programs or seeking employment.

Life after College

(1) Learning has many dimensions. Understanding how your new environment functions in terms of its expectations and culture sometimes requires more imagination, flexibility, maturity, and judgment than working through a course syllabus. This is true particularly, but not exclusively, in employment situations.

While doing a Fulbright program in Taiwan, Emily Choi, Cornell '14, wrote:

> I'm working in an environment (an elementary school) which I am most likely to never be in again; there are so many people I meet and work with on a daily basis who have such different opinions from me. I don't know how I manage to even work with them. The most important thing, though, is to learn how to communicate, whether it be through speech or through writing.

(2) If you are in graduate school, you are both a pre-professional and a beginner/freshman, but isn't this true in a new employment position? If you are working in a new position or in graduate school, you need to ask yourself both what you have learned that day that applies to your work *and* what else you have learned.

Describing her first year of graduate school, Becca Harrison, Cornell '14, observes:

> I'd say the biggest two things I'm struggling with now are (1) not "becoming my work" without as easy access to extra-curricular activities as in undergrad, and (2) learning how to read productively. By "read productively," I'm referring to learning to grapple with a volume of material very different than I have had to in the past. I'm discovering quite quickly that time doesn't exist to read books cover-to-cover like I was able to [do as an] undergrad, and am working to learn to effectively skim (without feeling guilty!).

(3) Whether you are in medical school, graduate school, or law school, or beginning a new career, time management is crucial. Keep a chart of how you are using your time, including recreational time. EMC – Every Minute Counts – will serve you well. No matter how much you enjoy your work, do not become your work. Be sure you do *not* become a workaholic without any life outside work/school.

(4) Remember that time is *not* money; time is time, and it is what you have on this earth. Every day do something that is fun and relaxing. Busy people are more likely to be happy people. In contrast to when you were in college, where the activities were there for the taking like a smorgasbord, after college you may have to take the initiative to find groups – athletic, fitness, drama, music, cooking, learning new skills, etc. – that interest you.

(5) Take care of yourself physically and emotionally. Be sure to get enough exercise and sleep. Eat healthily. If you have emotional issues, seek help. Substance abuse, including alcohol, is as much if not more of a possible distraction and danger in your post-college life as in your undergraduate years.

(6) Be a part of a supportive community of friends and family. Isolation and loneliness are not your friends. Keeping in touch with college friends or, if you are employed in a big city, living with friends is a good way to bridge your journey from college into a new world. Your community may come from an alumni association, a religious group, a volunteering commitment, an outdoor or nature group, a choir or orchestra, a book group, or any combination of these and others that I have left out.

Elliot Singer, Cornell '08, stresses

> the importance of networking. … Start early and network often. Do not be afraid to reach out to a stranger in a field in which one is interested and ask for

advice. The worst that can happen is that they either won't answer or won't be able to help. Every job I've gotten since Teach For America is by talking to someone who knew someone who knew someone, etc. Too often I think students these days rely on Internet postings for jobs instead of seeking opportunities other ways.

(7) In work and graduate school, use the academic, practical, and interpersonal skills that you have learned in college through classes and activities in which you have participated. Interpersonal skills help networking – and networking is useful in opening doors – but don't spend your life worrying about making connections. If you are involved in activities, networking will come.

(8) As always, speaking articulately, writing lucidly and precisely, reading carefully and thoughtfully, and thinking critically will serve you well.

(9) Understand that not everyone has had the same experiences as you have – indeed, everyone has had different experiences – and be open to learning from others. Balancing listening and speaking is an art form that needs to be learned. If you tend to be a talker, sometimes it is necessary to call a time-out on yourself and consciously not speak for a while.

(10) Develop new skills and interests – both in your professional and non-work life – even if you have limited time to cultivate them. Open the door to new experiences such as travel. If you are living in a city or visit one, try art museums, opera, ballet, and other cultural experiences that you may not have given much of chance.

(11) Be bold and take reasonable risks. Have a dream, but be sure it has roots in reality by being aware of your qualifications, abilities, and potential. Continue to develop new interests and new skills, including computer skills. Stay in touch with undergraduate professors whom you respect and who have an interest in you, and don't hesitate to seek their advice.

Post-graduate career counseling can be helpful if you become stuck and are thinking of a new direction. I know several students who decided as undergraduates to go to medical school after college and enrolled in courses and programs to make that possible. Bryn Mawr has an excellent post-graduate one-year pre-med program.

I conclude with three suggestions that are important at every stage of life:

(12) Remember the three Rs:

A) **Resilience: Falling down and getting up are one motion.**
B) **Resourcefulness: Use your skills and intelligence, while drawing upon your experience.**
C) **Resolve: Pursue goals with determination and persistence.**

(13) When things are not going well or you make mistakes, remember you usually can't fix the past. But you can start from where you are.

(14) Laugh a lot and continue to develop your sense of humor.

Part III
Further Essentials

9

Seventeen Suggestions for How to Choose Classes in College

In this chapter I will discuss how to choose classes, something that is very important to your using the resources of college to further your growth and development.

My suggestions are not in order of importance.

(1) Even while filling prerequisites and requirements for your major as well as distribution requirements during your first two years, each term – if time permits – take one class that expands your interests. In some cases, required distribution courses will be expanding your range of interests.

(2) After you choose a major, continue to take one course a term that expands your interests or develops necessary skills that complement your major. Even after fulfilling basic graduation requirements, STEM majors need to expose themselves to the humanities and social sciences; humanities majors need to take some basic sciences and social sciences; and students in the social sciences need to think about the humanities and sciences.

No matter what your major, you will need to develop tech skills. Every student needs to have a course in computer science and in economics, and every student needs to learn how to write lucidly and precisely and to learn how to use evidence to make a well-structured argument. Take as many courses as possible that require extended written assignments.

How to Succeed in College and Beyond: The Art of Learning, First Edition. Daniel R. Schwarz.
© 2016 John Wiley & Sons, Ltd. Published 2016 by John Wiley & Sons, Ltd.

Matt Barsamian, Cornell '04, observes:

> I strongly agree with your admonition that students should step outside their comfort zone. I believe I dropped Introduction to Microeconomics three times as an undergraduate and never wound up taking it. I still regret not doing so. College is a rare opportunity where you can learn just about anything, and it is very, very difficult to find the time and motivation to do so once you are working.

(3) During your four years in college, take classes that cultivate new interests. Try a class or two in creative writing, music, art, and/or theater. A basic survey course in these fields will give you an overview. Such classes will be an investment because they will prepare you for a lifetime of enjoyment.

In the humanities, where prerequisites are less important, a more specialized class may be more challenging and ultimately have a higher yield in terms of introduction to a field. Thus what you learn from an in-depth class on Mozart will carry over into your understanding of Beethoven or Brahms, and what you learn about seventeenth-century Dutch painting will help you understand the Italian Renaissance.

If you are not a scientist, take a class or two that enables you to understand such social and political issues as climate change, epidemics, population growth, genetic engineering and testing, and fossil fuels. At the very least you will be an informed citizen, but you may also have a chance in the future to shape policy on some of these issues within your community.

David DeVreis, Associate Dean of Undergraduate Education at the Cornell College of Arts and Sciences, concurs:

> [We need to] encourage students to extend their attention beyond the immediate task of the semester, asking them to think about the immediate within the context of the long-ranges of both collegiate and future life-paths. [It is especially important for students to take] courses in the arts in order to build for themselves a basis upon which a life-long appreciation can grow.

(4) Speaking to other students about a professor or classes is a valuable source of information, but it is important to know how serious and responsible your sources are. Keep in mind that the best teachers offer courses that are often demanding. If you know that such a splendid class outside your major must get less of your attention in terms of effort and commitment, you might take it using the pass/fail option rather than miss the learning experience.

(5) Sign up each term for as many courses as your school will allow and go to more classes the first week than you plan to take. After a few classes, you will have a good idea whether the class is for you. In addition, if need be, you can just go to larger classes without signing up. But where enrollment is limited, it is best to have your name on the initial list.

(6) On the whole, when possible, take professors not courses. Taking classes with engaged professors who love their subject and communicate both their passion and in-depth understanding is part of the joy of learning. Such professors can brighten an entire semester as well as the entire college experience.

(7) Find professors who are interested in their students and care about their students' growth. It may be reductive to say that some professors teach their subject, whereas others teach their subject to individual students, but there is a good deal of truth in that distinction.

As I have mentioned previously, the professors who ask you about your plan of study, your goals, your outside activities, and seem to care about you as a human being will not only be those you can go to for advice, but those who could provide a future reference for you.

(8) Remember, too, that no professor is the best professor for everyone. But in general, the best professors are those who expect you to come to every class prepared, take attendance, have high expectations, and give challenging assignments. The best professors not only read student assignments carefully and expeditiously but also prepare each student to do the assignments successfully.

(9) Take classes that emphasize concepts and how to apply them. Learning by rote is less important than learning how to think for yourself and to solve problems, both crucial qualities for your future. Of course, some classes, like those in first- or second-year foreign languages, do emphasize developing basic skills.

Learning how to think is a quality that develops in part from watching professors work through issues and synthesize on their feet when answering complex questions as well as understanding how they conceptualize assignments and exam questions. Most importantly, learning how to think involves solving problems and meeting challenges connected with papers and exams. In STEM courses, learning how to think involves responding to complex conceptual and theoretical issues as well as interpreting the evidence from experiments. James Phelan, Distinguished University Professor at Ohio State, observes:

> [It is important to recognize] the inextricable connections between learning-that and learning-how. Learning-that is about mastering bodies of knowledge, and learning-how is about being able to do things with what you've learned. Each is crucial, yet each is empty without the other. Those who get the most out of college recognize this point (either intuitively or consciously) and act accordingly.

The best professors typically exemplify the point – and, indeed, that's a big reason their classes are so interesting and worthwhile: they set up feedback loops between facts and skills, between learning-that and learning-how.

Be aware that some problems are intractable and vague, and courses that put everything in PowerPoint and neat packages are at times suspect. In your future career as a doctor, lawyer, government employee, or researcher, you will come upon problems that cannot be neatly solved or solved at all.

(10) A current buzzword is "metacognition." What that means is knowing about knowing, or knowledge about when and how to use particular strategies for learning or for problem solving. Thus, when writing a paper or pursuing a lab experiment or social science project, think about what you know, what you need to know, what you can't know, and how to use that mix to solve intellectually challenging problems and paradoxes.

Ryan Larkin, Cornell '14, observes:

> [Metacognition is] a concept that I've never really thought about before, but it's one that is absolutely essential to the practical work that I continue to do as a film student. A director of photography must always be ready to react to unexpected situations, and his ability to problem solve is directly related to how well he can deploy the strategies and knowledge at his disposal.

(11) Take courses that stress integrative learning, that enable you to understand material beyond one course, and to transfer what you have learned in one area to another area. If your course in Russian literature enables you to better understand Putin's aspirations and follies, you would be integrating your learning. Another example is reading di Lampedusa's masterwork *The Leopard*, not only for its literary value but to better understand Italian and Sicilian history, politics, and class divisions as well as the continuing economic tensions between Northern and Southern Italy. Using psychology, including psychoanalysis, to understand literary characters and their authors is another example of integrative learning. By combining science and economics, integrative learning can also help us understand the effects of climate change on future generations.

(12) Take courses where the professor can put material in context, references other fields, and has some knowledge of the world beyond the classroom. Through course selection, reading, and attending lectures, you need to keep informed about the world at large, including environmental and sustainability issues that affect us all, as well as how our government functions and how we can change it.

Follow international news and have a map of the world or a globe in your room and relate what you learn and read to specific places.

(13) Take courses that help make you aware of ethical and moral issues. You are preparing yourself for life, and such awareness will make you not only a better citizen, family member, and employee but also a better member of the campus community.

(14) Learn to think about the experiential implications of what you are learning because solving academic problems can carry over into other aspects of life. Conversely, find internships and campus activities that give you an experiential base for what you are learning. Depending on your field, this could take the form of working in a lab, as a museum guide (docent), for a university publication, or on the campus newspaper. Find summer internships and positions that enable you to integrate your knowledge with your experience.

(15) Supplement the classes in which you are enrolled with lectures by guest speakers, audits, and occasional visits to classes that you hear are stimulating. A professor will generally welcome guests.

(16) Take courses that require your participation. At best such courses become communities of inquiry, and communities require working together. Learning how to be part of a functioning group comes from small classes requiring participation.

In your career, you will need to work with people, and employers like people who can work in collaborative situations, who know the basics of teamwork, and who respond to the ideas of others even while sharing their own ideas.

(17) Because of the Internet, we live in a Global Village with virtually instant availability of news (as well as social gossip) as events occur and develop. While we cannot know what future technology will bring us, we do know that students need to take courses to prepare for continuing internationalization. Language skills are important, even if English has become the educated world's lingua franca, that is, its common language. If you want to be part of globalization – and you have no choice – you might think about learning Mandarin while in college, and if your focus will be the Americas, fluency in Spanish is necessary. Collaboration in research and business and social programs can depend on language fluency.

Conclusion

Discussion-oriented classes in which you learn to articulate your perspective and respond to the views of others are valuable not only for clarifying and refining your thinking, but also for developing essential tools for participating as a valued team member at work, in your avocations, and in the civic life of your community. Indeed, the give and take of ideas is what separates democracy from other forms of government.

10

The Greek System: Should You Join a Fraternity or Sorority?

Introduction: The Greek System in 2015

I begin with a question: Were the Greek system proposed today as a way of improving campus life for colleges and universities, would it be approved? I am convinced that at most colleges and universities, the answer would be "No." At Cornell, where I teach, with over 1,000 extra-curricular and service activities and a plethora of ways to find a comfortable community of friends, what would be the reason for approving such a system? Would anyone imagine the necessity of the Greek system in 2015 were it not here already?

Fraternities and sororities date to an era of campus parietal rules that governed men's interactions with women living in residential facilities. These rules have long since disappeared. They also date from a time when there were far fewer other activities on campus. The fraternities and sororities provided a social community and held the promise of valuable future business – mostly for men in the early days – and social contacts with those who belonged to chapters at other colleges of the same house.

At some point, major universities and colleges that still retain the Greek system will need to consider whether the Greek system, on balance, still serves a useful purpose or is an anachronism from a different time. This is particularly relevant at those universities and colleges that offer many opportunities for social interaction, community service, and leadership, all of which draw upon various student abilities and fulfill a multitude of students' interests and needs.

I believe fraternities and sororities have outlived their usefulness. Were they proposed today, administrators, professors, and hosts of students would agree that

How to Succeed in College and Beyond: The Art of Learning, First Edition. Daniel R. Schwarz.
© 2016 John Wiley & Sons, Ltd. Published 2016 by John Wiley & Sons, Ltd.

leadership could be developed in hundreds of existing groups. These groups include athletic teams (varsity, club, and intramural sports), student government, religious organizations, and political clubs, as well as campus publications, musical groups (band, orchestra, a cappella singing, etc.), and dance and theater groups.

Fraternities and sororities tend to breed homogeneity and conformity in the form of shared social, ethical, and political attitudes and behavior. Many of them encourage alcohol consumption, and that often includes underage and illegal drinking. Finally, they absorb time that could be better spent on academic work and extra-curricular activities, including community service. Because of these factors, Greek organizations may at times reduce student innovation and creativity. From my observation, fraternities and, to a lesser extent, sororities impose a kind of conformity that stifles growth and creates anxiety about being different or not going along with accepted mores.

Here is a fair question for students to ask: In terms of personal growth, which includes developing independent views, is it better to live in a dorm or residential college where there is more economic and social diversity and where getting along does not mean subscribing to the views of your fraternity brothers or sonority sisters?

According to then Cornell President David Skorton in his August 23, 2011 *New York Times* article "A Pledge to End Fraternity Hazing": "At Cornell, high-risk drinking and drug use are two to three times more prevalent among fraternity and sorority members than elsewhere in the student population."

In light of that statistic and my other objections, I doubt that the Greek system is worth maintaining and believe Cornell and other universities and colleges should (a) take the bold step of looking into alternatives; and/or (b) use instances of fraternity misbehavior – and sorority misbehavior, which occurs much less often – to permanently eliminate the offending houses one by one and use the buildings for something like the very successful Cornell undergraduate residential college system that has been instituted as an alternative. I am a house fellow at one of the residential colleges at Cornell; here the students are more diverse than those in the Greek system, hazing does not exist, and there is a rich intellectual life complemented by social activities.

Dartmouth

Dartmouth students have become increasingly impatient with the Greek system. Writing about Dartmouth on August 13, 2014, Tyler Kingkade, *Huffington Post* Senior Editor, reports:

> More than four times as many people suggested the Greek system was a problem than those who said it was not. In addition to the roughly 260 who said it should

be abolished, dozens of others called on the college to increase regulation or to require all houses to go coed.

A frontpage editorial in the October 17, 2014 Dartmouth student newspaper called for abolishing the Greek system:

> Let's do what needs to be done, the only action in line with our principles of community, and abolish the Greek system. ... For many, Greek life takes precedence over academics. It is an investment (perhaps a risky one), a path to acceptance, friends, sex, drugs, love, and jobs. Since so many students' lives seemingly depend on the system, it's no wonder that administrators have failed to abolish it, despite the numerous accounts of hazing and abuse that have been documented over the years. ... The Greek system undeniably enables and institutionalizes harmful behaviors.
>
> No, Greek life is not the root of all the College's problems or of broader societal ills. But as a system, it amplifies students' worst behavior. It facilitates binge drinking and sexual assault. It perpetuates unequal, gendered power dynamics and institutionalizes arbitrary exclusivity. It divides students – the system as a whole separates freshmen from upperclassmen, men from women. Membership draws lines among friends. ... .
>
> Many attribute increased confidence levels and better leadership and management skills to their Greek houses. We do not seek to discredit the positive experiences that many have within Greek spaces. But we cannot let emotional arguments cloud what is objectively best for our school and its students. We have to look past our short years here and think about the College's future, which means eliminating an antiquated system. Abolishing Greek life, though not a be-all, end-all solution, would offer Dartmouth a chance to rebuild its social life from the ground up.

Some months later, Dartmouth President Philip Hanlon announced a ban on hard liquor and that Dartmouth was monitoring the behavior and role of the Greek system (see Richard Pérez-Peña, "Dartmouth Cites Student Misconduct on Its Ban on Hard Liquor").

According to a 2014 *Bloomberg Review* editorial:

> Although a majority of college students drink, abusive drinking is far more prevalent in fraternities. One study of 17,000 students at 140 four-year colleges found that almost 90 percent of fraternity house residents engage in binge drinking (five or more drinks at a time), compared with 45 percent for nonmembers. Binge drinking is associated with a host of ills, from neurological damage to assaults.
>
> Alcohol abuse also plays a central role in one of the most corrosive aspects of fraternities: hazing of new members in initiation rituals that are often brutal and vile. ...
>
> The anti-intellectualism that dominates so much of fraternity life – the frat-boy culture of spring-break lore and "Animal House" – also takes a toll on its

members' academic performance. Even adjusting for differences in ability, age, and other factors, fraternity members tend to have lower grades and under-perform compared with their nonmember peers in tests of cognitive skills.

Fraternities also are at cross-purposes with the goal of promoting campus diversity. As a whole, they are more homogenous than the overall college student population.

Why Does the Greek System Survive?

The Greek system thrives for many reasons, but an important one is its emphasis on college partying, which – along with other demands the Greek system makes on its members – results in a substantial decline in study time. (Study time is the inclusive term for class preparation, homework, paper writing, and exam study.) For some students, fraternities and sororities become extremely time-consuming and replace a focus on academic study or other activities. The Greek system often encourages a kind of sectarianism in which membership in the fraternity or sorority takes precedence over commitment to the larger community.

While residential colleges and universities have always had a social compo-nent, that component seems to be greater now; of course, partying varies from school to school. Certainly some of the partying – taking place even on week-days, with Thursday being a particular focus – derives from the Greek system, where beer can be accessible 24/7.

Why has this occurred? Why have some college administrators and trustees allowed colleges to be turned into party circuses on weekends and sometimes during the week? Why do they turn a blind eye to underage drinking and, on occasion, use of illegal substances? Why do they fail to acknowledge that sexual harassment and abuse as well as demeaning and dangerous hazing are rampant on campuses? Often these issues are generated by the Greek system, particularly fraternities.

One answer to the questions above is that administrators and trustees are fol-lowing the money. They are supporting a system that attracts students and, they hope, will turn some of the wealthy and financially successful students into donors. They believe that this partying culture is what many students want and why they choose a particular college, as well as in some cases why they choose a particular Greek system "party house" in which such behavior is encouraged.

Many students attend colleges with social activities – the prospect of "having a blast" – uppermost in their minds. Students spend grant and loan money on bar bills and social activities that have little to do with education. Once rowdy drinking parties revolved around fraternity and sorority tailgating events at football and basketball games, but at some large universities these campus-wide celebrations are now held for almost any event or holiday.

With many less competitive colleges eager, if not desperate, for students to enroll and to pay soaring tuition, fraternities and sororities serve that goal by attracting some students who might not otherwise be in college. It should be noted that some of the soaring expenses of major universities derive from their competitive need to turn their dormitories and dining halls into those of a three-star resort and their athletic facilities into those of an Olympic site. Remodeled and new Greek houses can also add to the student costs.

As Caitlin Flanagan puts it in her March 2013 cover story in *The Atlantic* entitled "The Dark Power of Fraternities": "[F]raternities provide colleges with unlimited social programming of a kind that is highly attractive to legions of potential students, most of whom are not applying to ivy-covered rejection factories, but rather to vast public institutions and obscure private colleges that are desperate for students." I have been told by students at various schools that they would not have attended a school without a Greek system, but when I ask Cornellians if they would have turned down Cornell for another school or chosen not to apply were there no fraternities or sororities, they never answer yes to either question.

Issues to Consider Before You Join the Greek System

The Greek System, the Party Culture, and the Nature of the College Educational Experience

It would be unfair to put the predominant blame for the decrease in study time on the Greek system. But the demands of the Greek system – including the pledging period and, later, compulsory meetings as well as various activities and expectations – may contribute to the decline in study time.

Even if the evidence is not clear about whether Greek students study less or get lower grades – and I have found studies both pro and con – the cost in hours is excessive. Some of the Greek social activities, like older sorority sisters making by hand silly required gifts for their younger or "little sisters," and vice versa, not only are time consuming, but seem more appropriate for 12 year olds than for mature young adults. Other required gifts are simply financially costly.

All too few college students think of their education as a full-time job requiring an investment of time out of class equal in hours to twice the credit hours. This formula for study time was once considered the basic rule of thumb for college success; certainly this was true in 1959–63 when I was an undergraduate. Two hours per credit is still the standard I use for independent study courses.

According to a 2011 interview with Richard Arum and Josipa Eokas for NPR ("A Lack of Rigor Leaves Students 'Adrift' in College"): "[T]here has been a 50 percent decline in the number of hours a student spends studying and preparing for classes from several decades ago." They speculate that

> [O]ne possible reason for a decline in academic rigor and, consequentially, in writing and reasoning skills, is that the principal evaluation of faculty performance comes from student evaluations at the end of the semester. Those evaluations, Arum says, tend to coincide with the expected grade that the student thinks he or she will receive from the instructor.

In one 2011 research project, college students averaged 15 hours a week of study time, with engineers averaging 19 hours, and those in the social sciences and business averaging 14 hours (Karen Herzog, "Survey"). A 2014 study puts the average at 17 hours (Kathy Pierre, "How Much Do You Study?"). I have seen numbers as low as 10 to 13 hours ("Is Your College Student Investing Enough Time Studying?" on the College Parent Central website). Some schools still recommend 2 hours per week for every credit hour, but this recommendation seems not to be taken seriously by most students at most schools. In fact, I have discovered that most current students have never heard of it.

At Many Colleges, Significant Social Problems Are Associated with the Greek System

In some places, as Caitlin Flanagan observes in "The Dark Power of Fraternities":

> [F]raternities are now mightier than the colleges and universities that host them. ... The organizations raise millions of dollars for worthy causes, contribute millions of hours in community service, and seek to steer young men toward lives of service and honorable action. They also have a long, dark history of violence against their own members and visitors to their houses, which makes them in many respects at odds with the core mission of college itself.

Hardly a week goes by without a report of an alcohol-related death or a story about date rape or other abusive misbehavior taking place at a fraternity, and often nothing more occurs than a ritualistic announcement from the school administration about "deep regret" and "looking into the incident." Outrageous misbehavior occurs, in part, because many fraternities demean women by thinking of them as sexual objects, and that stereotyping can lead at worst to non-consensual sexual behavior. We have ample evidence that fraternities and sororities are sites of more frequent anti-social behavior than is the case for any other sites where students live.

Let me cite some data:

> According to the US Department of Education's Higher Education Center, 75% of fraternity members engaged in heavy drinking, compared with 49% of other male students. Likewise, 62% of sorority members engaged in binge drinking versus 41% of non-sorority members. … More students engaged in drinking at fraternity and sorority houses than any other on-campus venue or residence hall. According to the Harvard School of Public Health's College Alcohol Study, 75% of students living in fraternity and sorority houses were heavy drinkers, compared to 45% of students who lived in non-Greek housing and 35% of the overall student population. (Zen College Life, "15 Frightening Facts About Sororities and Fraternities")

On the same site are the assertions that more sexual assaults occur in fraternities than at other sites and that the most likely victims at fraternities are sorority members. The journal *Sex Roles* has shown that fraternity men are more likely to display images that objectify women and to believe women want to engage in rough sexual acts.

Other Greek Life Issues

Before joining the Greek system, you also need to consider the financial and personal costs. In an October 28, 2014 *New York Times* piece, "Greek Letters at a Price," Risa C. Doherty offers an interesting perspective on the hidden costs of joining a sorority. Not only are there monthly or semester dues, but there are house fees and various social expenditures incurred by social activities and big sister (or brother) relationships with incoming little sisters (or brothers); these expenditures for both younger and older students can be in the hundreds of dollars. One parent claims to have spent over $3,200 in the student's first year (Julie and Lindsey Mayfield, "7 Considerations When Thinking About Greek Life").

Since fraternities and sororities tend to choose members who are like themselves, they tend to contribute to campus ethnic and socio-economic divisions. They often become enclaves where similar political views, social codes, and economic status prevail. Often the fraternities and sororities focus more on social occasions – mixers – than on serious issues. Rarely do campus protests against social injustices originate in the Greek system. Historically, fraternities have been less than tolerant of homosexuals and at worst have encouraged homophobia.

Another significant downside of the Greek system is that students who do not get chosen by the more prestigious houses often question their self-worth, and those not chosen at all feel ostracized. Moreover, the selection process often does not measure intellect, social maturity, or ethics, but physical attractiveness, economic status, and "fitting in" to the existing house culture and mores. Of course, one could argue with some cynicism that not getting everything we want when we want it is good preparation for life, but that does not alleviate painful disappointment.

Abusive hazing polices associated with initiation have at times resulted in injuries and even deaths. But we do need to remember that hazing is not restricted to fraternities and sororities. Varsity teams, especially male ones, and college bands have also been implicated in abusive incidents and unacceptable behavior that jeopardize the health of students.

My advice to students: If anyone asks you to do something that is abusive, compromises your dignity, or negatively affects your physical or emotional health and sense of self in the name of pleasing someone or creating commitment to a group – whether it be a fraternity, sorority, team, or other group – walk away immediately.

The Pro-Fraternity Counter-Argument (and Some Responses to That Argument)

Let us turn to reasons proposed for joining the Greek system, and also consider their validity.

Travis Apgar, Associate Dean of Students, and the person directly in charge of Cornell Greek life, claims: "The leadership, self-governance, integrity, and interpersonal skills that are developed, combined with the outside of the classroom educational experiences such as community service opportunities is what makes belonging so special."

I have learned from students that the main advantage of membership in the Greek system is that belonging overcomes a sense of loneliness and gives students a sense of being part of a community that cares about them. In a sense it breaks down the campus – particularly that of a large university with many lecture classes numbering in the hundreds – into smaller, manageable units. Many members form lifetime friendships.

Many students and alumni believe fraternities and sororities do enrich the lives of young adults. They provide a community and may give students a chance to take on a leadership role within the community. Proponents of the Greek system believe that fellow fraternity and sorority members from other colleges and universities provide an important networking base and will be more likely to hire them or recommend them for membership in prestigious social and community groups. Although local networking can be found in other extra-curricular campus activities as well as in various other living arrangements, these networks are limited to individual campuses and graduates.

By contrast, the Greek system's network extends into the much larger social and business world of graduates of all chapters of a particular sorority or fraternity. However, in today's world, with its emphasis on merit, skills, and diversity, I am not sure this "old boy" network is as important as it once was, especially for employment.

Another argument I hear is that fraternities and sororities do worthwhile philanthropic work and community outreach, and such outreach can add to a CV. In recent years, notwithstanding the strong position of the Greek system on some campuses, many other organizations have developed to involve students in the community. In fact, involvement in other organizations has become a crucial part in CV building. Furthermore, Greek members have told me that in fact little time is devoted to community outreach and claims of philanthropic activity are mostly window-dressing.

I have often been told by students – including by some who excelled academically – how much the fraternity and sorority system meant to them, particularly in the second term of their freshman year and their sophomore year. However, I have also been told by many students that in junior and senior years, more students – and in my view some of the very best students – feel that fraternities and sororities are a tad claustrophobic and thus seek a wider variety of friends and activities. My advice: If you do join, be sure you participate in at least one other campus activity, and do not let your fraternity or sorority became the focal point of your college life.

Knowing of my skepticism about the Greek system in 2014, my honors thesis student Christian Kinsella, Cornell '14, observes: "I appreciate [your] acceptance that fraternities do work for some. I agree that they are not necessary or even ideal, but my diverse group of friends from Cornell would have been non-existent without Zeta Beta Tau (I know this is contrary to the norm, where fraternities perpetuate separatism)." Camille Finn, Cornell '15, adds:

> [T]he most valuable thing I have gotten out of my sorority experience has been the lifelong friends that I have made. My first semester at Cornell was very hard and I didn't have many friends; I felt pretty lonely at times. When I joined a sorority second semester I began to feel a sense of belonging here, and the enjoy-ment that I got out of the sorority [was] reflected in my overall happiness and success at Cornell. The network of people that a sorority gives you includes girls from different backgrounds who share your same values and interests, and alumni who truly care about developing a personal connection with you and the sorority. You can definitely find these things through different organizations and venues at Cornell, but my sorority has given me many irreplaceable experiences that have shaped my growth as a person at this school and beyond.

I have indicated in the preceding pages why I am skeptical that the experiences she values could not be found elsewhere.

Another argument in favor of the Greek system that I often hear is that major alumni donors would be offended if the Greek system were abolished, in part because their allegiance is as much or more to their fraternities and sororities than to the university. However, I have known and know many of the major givers to Cornell, and I am most doubtful that their interest in the university derives from fraternity affiliation. Were Cornell to abolish the Greek system, there would be some alumni dissatisfaction and grumbling, but I would argue that the long-term gain in campus civility and community would more than offset the loss in funds, and that any temporary financial loss would come not from the foremost givers but from secondary ones. Most of the trustees and principal donors think of themselves as representing Cornell and not their fraternities and sororities, if they belonged to one. To an extent, these individuals and families think of themselves as custodians for the life and future welfare of the university as a whole.

Yet another argument against abolishing the Greek system here and elsewhere is that it would leave colleges and universities without enough housing, especially since they do not own many of the buildings housing fraternities and sororities. I have looked into this at Cornell. Of the 39 fraternity residences at Cornell, about a third are owned by the university. The rest are owned or rented by the fraternities and sororities. But if the Greek system were abolished, the fraternities and sororities that own their houses would have little choice except to sell their houses to Cornell, which could then use most of them as residences and perhaps a few houses for some other function.

Landlords who rent houses to fraternities or sororities could just as easily rent them to the university or individual students – or sell the houses to Cornell. That houses on campus cannot be sold to a commercial enterprise, and that those houses off campus are zoned as residential, would limit if not prevent the possibility of sales to businesses. Cornell could buy those that they do not own and turn them into college residences or sites for academic programs, although campus housing needs probably would demand the former.

What Happens If the Greek System Is Abolished?

Travis Apgar, the aforementioned Cornell Associate Dean of Students in charge of the Greek system, argues that it would take less effort and money to improve the Greek system than to abolish it, but I am doubtful that he is right.

Colleges that have abolished the Greek system, such as Middlebury, Amherst, Williams, and Colby, are hardly immune to such social problems as excessive drinking and sexual harassment. But the administrators of these colleges do think they are better off without the Greek system (Zach Schonfeld, "Inside the Colleges That Killed Frats for Good").

Apparently, a small number of students at some of the aforementioned colleges belong to so-called underground fraternities. Indeed, Amherst as of July 1, 2014 threatened to expel or suspend all the 90 (of a student body of 1,800) students who belonged to underground fraternities (Paige Sutherland, "Amherst Cracks Down on Fraternities, Sororities").

Conclusion

While not dismissing the positive role that fraternities and sororities have played and do play for some students, my advice is to be wary of the Greek system and alert to the alternatives in terms of living arrangements and sources of friendship. I have known many students whose initial enthusiasm waned but who were afraid to deactivate lest they would be ostracized by their former brothers and sisters. Do not join a fraternity or sorority simply because a few friends are joining; if they are real friends, you will not lose them. If you are thinking about joining, consider "dry" houses where alcohol is not permitted. For some students, waiting until their sophomore year gives them time to think more maturely about joining rather than simply following the herd as freshmen. Ask yourself whether your student life will be richer if you try a few terms without the Greek system. You may find by your sophomore year that you have discovered other resources and don't need that system at all.

11

More Thoughts on the College Experience: Brief Observations and Suggestions

In this chapter I will expand on some matters I have touched on earlier, as well as add some new ideas.

Time Management: Using Your Time Efficiently and Effectively

If any one thing determines success in school and in life, it is time management. Because time is your most valuable and malleable commodity, rather than think "Time is money," think "Time is time." How you use time will define you.

Some of what I propose below is also scattered through other chapters, but I thought it would be useful to pull it together.

(1) I suggest keeping an hour-by-hour chart – at least for a while – so that you know how you are using your time. You should also have a weekly and even a monthly plan, knowing that it may have to be amended several times in the face of events. Keeping a calendar is essential so that you don't miss appointments and deadlines.

(2) You need to have a number of specific places where you study effectively outside your dorm room if you live on campus. Even if you live in a single room, noise and fellow students stopping by can be distractions.

How to Succeed in College and Beyond: The Art of Learning, First Edition. Daniel R. Schwarz.
© 2016 John Wiley & Sons, Ltd. Published 2016 by John Wiley & Sons, Ltd.

(3) You need a regular routine for doing your academic work. When you awaken – or before you go to bed – think about how your day will be going in terms of time, including how much time you will be spending on extra-curricular activities (sports, university publications, music practice, theater rehearsal, debate) as well as employment if you have a job.

(4) If you have time between classes, learn how to use that time efficiently. If you have a 50-minute class at 9:05 that ends at 9:55 and another that begins at 11:15, use those 80 minutes productively.

(5) Let me repeat an important Basic Rule: no time period is too short to accomplish something. Especially when you are writing about something that you have been thinking about for a while, a 15- or 20-minute block of time accompanied by a burst of creativity can often produce results equal to those produced in longer time periods.

(6) Be aware of how much time you spend with your smartphone, email, and social media. If you are in a relationship, be aware of how much time it is taking.

(7) Be aware of how much time you spend on social activities, including conversations with friends that stretch on for hours. Being a good friend is important, but beware of being the scoutmaster or den mother for every problem that arises among the people you know well.

(8) In general, if you are at an elite college or university, 10 or 12 hours will be as much as you can work on a paid job without hurting your academic performance, but at less demanding colleges and universities, many students – notably older students – do carry a full course load and work longer hours. As I have noted, the traditional rule for study time at an elite college is two hours study outside of class for every hour in class, although, depending on your program, ability, and other commitments, you may do more and many do less.

(9) Do something that is fun every day, whether it be walking in the woods or in your neighborhood, or playing pick-up basketball or volleyball, or stopping by at the university museum, etc.

(10) Learn the value of alone time; this is when you can digest what is happening in your life.

Essential Skills for Succeeding in College and Beyond

In your college years, stress the development of crucial skills: writing effectively, speaking articulately, thinking critically, studying with focus, working well with others, as well as computer literacy and economic intelligence.

The Art of Writing Well

Writing effectively requires continuous practice. You need to strive for precision and clarity. Focus on expanding your vocabulary and sentence variety. Learn how to present an argument. Be attentive to the prose you read and be aware of the differences among kinds of journalism – investigative journalism, news coverage, and feature writing. Understand the various ways that evidence and argument are presented in various fields: for example, scientific writing often requires passive voice while other kinds of argument require active voice.

Keeping a daily journal supplements course assignments. It can be useful to write even a handful of thoughtful sentences about your course readings and in-class discussions and the ideas they generate. If you wish, you can alternate educational entries with personal entries. But in both cases, be sure to be attentive to style and grammar; seek the best possible syntax and diction to present your thinking. Writing requires drafts; you need to begin assignments soon after they are assigned so you have time to revise and polish your work.

Two recommended texts: Strunk and White's *The Elements of Style* for crucial advice in a succinct form and the *Hodges Harbrace Handbook* (edited by Cheryl Glenn and Loretta Gray) for basic usage, grammar, and punctuation advice such as when to use commas, colons, and semi-colons.

Speaking Articulately and Forcefully

For some, speaking in class is a pleasure and something at which they excel. For others, it is their worst nightmare. For most, it is in between the two.

You might try recording yourself to see how you sound and whether you are speaking logically, succinctly, and to the point. Even if you think you excel in classroom discussion, you might try recording yourself because you may be surprised at the number of pauses, "ums," and "you knows" that you use.

If you have trouble speaking in class, you might try writing down what you want to say and glancing at it while you speak.

Classes in public speaking and acting as well as membership in debating clubs are ways of developing speaking skills. Taking leadership positions that require public speaking to a group can also help. Prepare for oral reports by rehearsing what you are going to say and, if possible, don't read your notes. Learning how to muster evidence to support your point of view and displaying confidence when giving oral presentations are important to future success in most endeavors. Learning how to integrate slides, photographs, and videos into your presentations – whether you use PowerPoints or not – is important. Rather than imitate any one person, develop your own style by being attentive to a variety of good public speakers.

Critical Thinking

You need to learn how to think rather than what to think. As you read and listen to teachers and classmates, you should be thinking, "Is this true?" "Is it always true?" "Has all the evidence been presented?" "Can I make a counter-argument?" "Can I make the point being argued more nuanced?"

Studying with Focus

Learning how to study efficiently and to concentrate are important skills in college and beyond. An essential study skill is learning how to take useful notes in and outside of class. Studying takes many forms, from reading slowly for the purpose of retaining information to sifting through large bodies of material to get an overview. Studying includes reading and writing to develop ideas and understand issues. Studying also includes doing problem sets and lab reports as well as planning and completing papers for formal assignments.

One problem is that many students do not develop study skills in high school, so that time spent studying in college is not fruitful. Two important variables in college success are how much students study and how well they use their study time.

Attention to social media deflects contemporary students from their academic work. One 2014 study reported by Janice Wood (which I find somewhat preposterous), claims that female college students are spending 8 to 10 hours and men a little less than 8 hours with their smartphones. Other studies (e.g. "Is Your College Student Investing Enough Time Studying?" on the College Parent Central website) show that students who drink less spend less time studying and that some students spend more time drinking than they do studying.

Learning How to Work with Others

More and more, industry and universities are stressing human relationships in the workplace and how well people work within a group or within a team. Difficult people waste the time of other people. Collaborative and positive work environments not only leave employees feeling good about themselves and developing loyalty to their employers, but also are far more productive.

Computer Literacy

Because we live in a digital age, the more you are conversant with how computers work and what they can do, the better. Programming skills will help you in academic work, job searches, and career development. I recommend that every student take a basic course in computer science, either at the high school or college level or both.

Understanding Economics

Understanding how the economy functions and why and how numbers matter in terms of inflation, unemployment, interest rates, gross national product, and other barometers is crucial to your personal financial well-being and to any business in which you have an interest, even as an employee. Every college student needs to take a course in economics.

Athletic Scholarships, Athletic Illusion and Delusion

Recruiting and scholarship rules for US college athletics are governed by the NCAA, although each of its three Divisions – and even each athletic conference – has its own rules and regulations. For example, the Ivy League where I teach has somewhat stricter recruiting rules than other Division I schools and is the only Division I conference that doesn't offer athletic scholarships.

If you want to play a college varsity sport, you need to find a school at which you not only make the team but also play in games. My son played varsity tennis at Cornell at a time when the Ivy League tennis teams were not as good as they are now. Had he been at Stanford, he would have been in the stands watching the matches.

At some schools, athletes – especially in major sports – are virtual employees of the universities, and they are encouraged to let their academic programs take a back seat to representing the school on the field or court. If you have athletic talent in revenue-producing sports like football and basketball and are on an athletic scholarship, you may be offered bogus courses and opportunities to cut corners, perhaps even to violate NCAA rules. Doing so is not in your long-term interest and may compromise your reputation. To some coaches, particularly at schools giving athletic scholarships, the physical and mental health of the player can be less important than winning. To be sure, such coaches are in the minority but they definitely exist.

Be aware of the time commitment varsity sports require, especially for those who are on athletic scholarship in a major sport. Before grade inflation, the informal accepted wisdom was that on average a varsity athlete sacrificed about

0.5 per term on his or her GPA. Now, the cost in terms of GPA may be less, but be sure that you spend considerable time studying and that you take – and attend – challenging classes and do your own work.

A student-athlete's illusion or delusion – often shared by parents and college coaches – of being on the road to professional stardom can lead to spending excessive time training and working out as well as taking easy courses, failing to attend classes regularly, and accepting "tutoring" that is not really tutoring but rather having someone else do the student's work.

Because very few athletes become professionals, a basic rule is: Don't sacrifice academics for athletics. Another reason for following this advice – even if you become one of the tiny percentage of men and women who make a living from your athletic ability – is that you will enjoy the world you live in more fully if you are well educated. You will have something to fall back on when your athletic career is over or if you are injured early in your career.

Advice to parents: You need to be wary of coaches – particularly coaches you have hired in individual sports like tennis and golf – who overestimate your children's ability and potential. In tennis more and more parents are realizing that to be highly ranked as a high school junior does not mean a professional career when so many countries have rankings and players training to be professionals. Beware of coaches in any sport who, for whatever reason, think your child is better positioned for stardom than in fact he or she might be.

Before signing a professional contract, students and parents need consider whether the student-athlete is really going to succeed as a professional or whether continuing education until graduation is a better alternative. Remember that agents get commissions on signed contracts and may not be counted on for the best advice.

Your Life Narrative

As you evolve, your narrative – the story you tell yourself about your past, present, and future – will change in the face of new experiences. But that story can also be a journey towards your goals.

Adjusting your life narrative is a continuous process that begins at an early age when you begin to realize that you probably are not going to be a professional athlete or a world-class violinist and that, while you can improve at almost anything, your choices are limited by your mental and physical aptitudes and sometimes by your physical stature.

It is important that the narrative you tell yourself reflects reality. Thus, if your story is about going to medical school in the future, choosing a particular medical field, and becoming a doctor in that field, you will need to begin taking the necessary science courses in high school and continue taking the more demanding college science courses that medical school requires. You may find delight in research and decide to combine a Ph.D. and MD, or perhaps even decide to do research in a particular science and become a professor.

Your story may be about becoming an elementary school teacher, but as you graduate and become engaged, not only in your teaching but in thinking about how a school should be organized, you may decide to go into school administration and become a principal or even a superintendent of schools. Or while heading into your family clothing or farming business, you may discover that you wish to become an engineer or a journalist.

College successes and failures will affect your narrative. You may find that you are not suited for your major or first career choice or that you are drawn to something else more powerfully than your original choices. Later, marriage, children, aging parents, the ill health of immediate family members, the need for greater earnings, or the need to accommodate your spouse's career aspirations can change your life narrative.

My point is that you need to be fully aware of how your narrative is evolving. One method is to keep a journal, either daily or weekly, in which you trace your progress toward your goals, consider whether your goals are consistent and attainable, and reflect on whether these goals are changing. Of course, your private life will play a role in your narrative; issues of finance, domestic stability or instability, motivation, and ability will be part of the process of re-examining your proposed narrative.

12

Growing Young Adults: What Parents Need to Know About Their Children in College

Following the publication of my *Huffington Post* columns on what students need to know about the college experience, I have been asked about what parents need to know.

(1) Your son or daughter is in college as an individual, not as part of the family team. While you want to be supportive and give advice when asked, you are not captain or coach of your student's team. That role belongs to your offspring, namely the student enrolled in college.

If you have overly managed your child's high school career and created anxiety preceding and during the college admission process, this is your chance to redress prior mistakes and be encouraging without being overbearing.

Let your student, now a young adult, solve his or her own problems. If you have raised your son or daughter well, he or she will have the confidence to make good decisions, but like all of us, your student will make mistakes and experience disappointments and learn from them. You need to encourage your son or daughter to remember the three Rs – resilience, resolve, and resourcefulness – and perhaps practice them yourself in regard to your college student rather than showing your own anxiety, disappointment, and frustration.

College students are young adults and need to take the initiative to solve roommate issues, housing problems, course registration, and challenging assignments. It may be hard to let go, but what college should be doing is turning adolescents into adults who make decisions, and if you intervene that will not happen. (I recommend Marshall Duke, "Starting College: A Guide for Parents: 2013.")

How to Succeed in College and Beyond: The Art of Learning, First Edition. Daniel R. Schwarz.
© 2016 John Wiley & Sons, Ltd. Published 2016 by John Wiley & Sons, Ltd.

(2) As much as you want to share this experience, hovering over your son or daughter (what is known as being a helicopter parent) is not the best way to help him or her grow. I advise limiting calls and emails so that your student has a sense of being on his or her own. Giving occasional advice if asked is ok, but it is often best to hold your tongue and, especially, control your desire to write emails every day or, as is the case with some parents, several times a day. While one rule does not fit all, calling more than once a week is excessive, and so is emailing or, even worse, phoning more than a few times a week. To be omnipresent is not the best way to be either helpful or close.

But you do want to listen to your son or daughter to be sure your student is pursuing goals for the future and taking his or her academic work seriously. Too much talk by the student about partying, homecoming, fraternity and sorority social life and not enough about courses is a warning sign. While extra-curricular activities are fun, and in some cases – acting in plays, writing for the school news-paper, and, in rare cases, playing on college teams – are part of professional goals, you do need to notice when these activities begin to take precedence over academic study.

One of the best ways to share the college experience is visiting when your son or daughter is competing on varsity teams, acting in a play, or being part of a musical performance. But on these occasions, it is important not to give too much advice to him or her, or, worse yet, *any* advice to the coach or the theater or musical director. These are the very occasions for parental restraint.

(3) However, you know your son or daughter, and if he or she is showing signs of depression or anxiety or panic – rather than the usual complaining about how much he or she has to do or how his or her roommate is inconsiderate, etc. – then you should contact the college's psychological services or the advising center. Unless you feel it is a life-threatening emergency, I would not rush to campus.

(4) As much as you are tempted, do not do your son's or daughter's academic work. It is time to let go. At the same time, your young student may want to share the excitement of his or her academic work. Especially if your son or daughter takes the initiative, discussion of course material and books he or she is reading can be mutually satisfying and may be helpful to your child. But this sharing is different from doing the student's assignments. In more cases than one might think, parents have been helping their student in high school, even doing homework and editing papers.

A few years ago I taught a freshman who had attended a private day school and had had so much help from parents – who also provided tutors for courses in which she was an A student – that doing her own work was a major adjust-ment. In a different case, I had an honors student who let her father edit her thesis after I had signed off on it; the father systematically turned active voice into passive and made other "corrections" that resulted in a lower grade than the one she would have received.

(5) The first thing to be aware of is that you will not know as much as you think you know. No matter how often you email or phone your student, she or he – not you – is in control of the information flow. If the student is having trouble understanding material in courses, you may or may not be told, but if that trouble derives in part or completely from cutting classes, not doing homework, or failing to study for exams or to do the required work on papers, you may not be told at all. Such problems can be caused by depression, anxiety, or other mental health issues that the student may be reluctant to share.

Nor will your student fully share his or her experiments with alcohol, consensual sexual behavior, illegal substances, all-nighters, hazing, or what you may think of as simple foolishness like a group howling at the moon during finals or running ("streaking") across the quad with other students while wearing little or no clothing. Even students who commute and live at home are not going to share all their experiences with you.

Of course, we all like to think that it is the sons and daughters of others who experiment or do foolish things. Remember, too, that you did not share everything with your parents.

You need to be attentive to behavior that affects your child's physical and mental health, including binge drinking – the most common form of foolish behavior and one that can lead to bad decisions about sex. You need to be alert to your student's failure to give proper attention to course work because that can lead to academic failure and suspension.

(6) When your son or daughter returns from college, especially during the first few breaks from classes, he or she will be different and more independent, and, while this occasionally will be off-putting, this change is in most cases desirable. Warmly welcoming your offspring and celebrating holidays together will create important continuity. But trying to recreate during these visits what once was is a mistake because your student has changed.

Moreover, expecting your son or daughter to spend the entire break with you is another mistake because he or she will want to catch up with high school friends and perhaps his or her college friends if they live nearby. If your student went to boarding school, you will be more used to these developments.

By the time your student is a senior, he or she may want to return to school early or visit friends rather than spend the four weeks between terms with you, and you should consider this as part of the process of both your child and you becoming independent adults.

(7) If your son or daughter is spending over his or her budget, and you are funding or partially funding college, you certainly have the right to express your concerns, since you are a financial partner. To a large extent, you have to trust your offspring and rely on his or her judgment. But on occasion, students, usually males, do get involved in costly foolishness like online gambling, and you need to question expenditures that seem excessive or inexplicable.

In many cases, particularly for freshmen, it is a good idea to have the student use a credit card for which you are co-owner and to check the expenditures.

(8) One site that further comments on the issues I have been discussing is College Parent Central (although be aware that this site advertises "advice" products and may be motivated by commercial interests). Another site is Campus ESP.

Conclusion

Sending your son or daughter to college should be an exhilarating experience, but it involves maturity and poise on your part. You need to restrain you desire to make everything right, fix every problem, or micro-manage your student's life. You want your college student to be independent and, if it is your only child or last child to leave home, you do not want to be compensating for your own "empty nest" issues.

Part IV
The Value of the Humanities

13

Why Study the Humanities?

Introduction

Following the 2013 report of the American Academy of Arts and Sciences on the crisis in the humanities entitled "The Heart of the Matter," I have seen quite a few insightful commentaries, most stressing economic utility – how the humanities help students succeed in whatever endeavor they pursue – and some stressing how the humanities contribute to making students better citizens in a democracy.

Moreover, as Adam Gopnik observes in an excellent August 2013 *New Yorker* piece, "Why Teach English?" "We need the humanities not because they will produce shrewder entrepreneurs or kinder CEOs but because … they help us enjoy life more and endure it better. The reason we need the humanities is because we're human."

In my definition, the humanities not only include literature of both ancient and modern languages, the performing arts, philosophy, history, comparative religion, and cultural studies, but also anthropology and linguistics, although the latter two are often on the border between the humanities and the social sciences.

What follows are my own reasons to study the humanities, with a particular focus on the arts. My reasons balance utility with more idealistic quality of life issues. Thus I want to stress both the *isness* and *doesness* of the humanities, which in fact is a version of the Horatian credo of delighting and instructing.

How to Succeed in College and Beyond: The Art of Learning, First Edition. Daniel R. Schwarz.
© 2016 John Wiley & Sons, Ltd. Published 2016 by John Wiley & Sons, Ltd.

Practical Value of the Humanities

On the utility or *doesness* side, I would stress the value of learning to think critically and independently, read powerfully and perceptively, write lucidly and precisely, and speak articulately. As David Brooks notes "Studying the humanities improves your ability to read and write. No matter what you do in life, you will have a huge advantage if you can read a paragraph and discern its meaning."

In a compelling April 16, 2015 *New York Times* piece, "Starving for Wisdom," Nicholas Kristof argues:

> [W]herever our careers lie, much of our happiness depends upon our interactions with those around us, and there's some evidence that literature nurtures a richer emotional intelligence. *Science* magazine published five studies indicating that research subjects who read literary fiction did better at assessing the feelings of a person in a photo than those who read nonfiction or popular fiction. Literature seems to offer lessons in human nature that help us decode the world around us and be better friends.
>
> Literature also builds bridges of understanding. Toni Morrison has helped all America understand African-American life. Jhumpa Lahiri illuminated immigrant contradictions. Khaled Hosseini opened windows on Afghanistan.
>
> In short, it makes eminent sense to study coding and statistics today, but also history and literature.

On October 4, 2014 the *Economist* published a piece advocating for business executives "inward-bound" courses that focus on reading great books instead of "outward-bound" courses focusing on physical prowess. In that piece the columnist known as Schumpeter argued:

> Inward-bound courses would do wonders for "thought leadership." ... [T]he only way to become a real thought leader is to ignore all this noise and listen to a few great thinkers. You will learn far more about leadership from reading Thucydides' hymn to Pericles than you will from a thousand leadership experts. You will learn far more about doing business in China from reading Confucius than by listening to "culture consultants." Peter Drucker remained top dog among management gurus for 50 years not because he attended more conferences but because he marinated his mind in great books: for example, he wrote about business alliances with reference to marriage alliances in Jane Austen. Inward-bound courses would do something even more important than this: they would provide high-flyers with both an anchor and a refuge.

Even more practical is the burgeoning field of digital humanities. As Paul Jay and Gerald Graff pointed out in a 2012 article:

> The emergence of this field calls attention to how old 20th-century divisions between science and the humanities are breaking down and gives those of us

committed to defending the practical value of the humanities a tremendous opportunity. The digital humanities represent the cutting-edge intersection of the humanities and computer science, the merging of skills and points of view from two formerly very different fields that are leading to a host of exciting innovations – and opportunities for students who want to enter fields related to everything from writing computer programs to text encoding and text editing, electronic publishing, interface design, and archive construction.

Mark Eisner, Cornell Ph.D. '70, who has a STEM background, but has done a considerable amount of editorial work, eloquently, if idealistically, observes:

(1) Humanities graduates can write, a critical skill in the workplace and one that many STEM graduates don't have. Proposals, funding pitches, progress reports, communications to the public, evaluations – all require the ability to put the right words together in clear sentences to tell a compelling story. The value of this skill is not limited to jobs with "communication" in the name. ...

(2) Humanities graduates can speak, another critical skill that STEM graduates often lack. Presentations, meetings, encounters with the public, one-on-one conversations – all require the ability to think on your feet and compose clear messages that advance the case.

(3) Humanities graduates can read, in a way that is different from the way many STEM graduates read. The ability to critically analyze texts is essential in reading proposals, [fully understanding] reports, and validating arguments.

(4) Humanities graduates can reason and analyze, digging down to figure out what is really going on and whether or not it makes sense. They can put detailed ideas into a broader context.

(5) Humanities graduates understand character, motivation, and ... social, historical, and moral [context]. They can be good "readers" of people, as effective managers must be.

(6) Humanities graduates have experience in a wide and diverse world, both through reading and through travel and association with other cultures. They can readily understand why different people – colleagues and customers – may respond differently as a consequence of the different worlds in which they live, and thereby relate to them effectively.

(7) Humanities graduates are creative. They can imagine outcomes and make them happen. I don't know whether consulting firms like McKinsey and Bain still seek creative people, but when [my daughter] Amy [Eisner, Harvard '94, who majored in English and American Literature and Language] was looking for her first job these firms were eager to hire her and others like her.

(8) Humanities graduates know how to listen, critically and compassionately.

Although a fervent advocate for the humanities, I would probably prefer to modify each of Eisner's eight claims with the word "sometimes." Certainly one can learn how to read and listen critically and compassionately without a graduate degree in the humanities.

What the Humanities Add to the Quality of Life

On the quality of life/joy of learning or *isness* side, I would stress that the arts take us into imagined worlds created by different minds and enable us to understand how others live. We are what we read, the museums we visit, and the performances we see and hear. They are as much us – part of our memories, our *isness* – as the culture we inherit and the life experiences we have.

That entry into other worlds and minds does give us a larger context for thinking about how to live and how to confront and understand present personal and historical issues, even while also giving us pleasure for its own sake.

Another way to think about what the arts do is to ask whether experiencing the arts makes us more perceptive and sensitive humans. We can say with some certainty that reading and viewing masterworks in the visual arts or in attending performances of great music, opera, or ballet widens our horizons about how people behave and what historical and cultural forces shape that behavior. But will, say, reading *War and Peace* be a catalyst to heroic action or even, as Tolstoy urges, putting family first if you have never done so? Probably not. Will it make us slightly more aware of the need to find definition and purpose in life? Perhaps in some nuanced, immeasurable way, the answer is "Yes." Do adolescents learn anything about life, love, and the place of the imagination from classic young adult fiction like Lawrence's *Sons and Lovers*, Joyce's *A Portrait of the Artist as a Young Man*, and Salinger's *The Catcher in the Rye*? I did.

Perhaps the best answer to who gets the most out of the arts is that it depends on what the reader, viewer, or listener brings to his or her experience. For there is a symbiotic relationship between art and audience, and each perceiver is a community of one. Or, as Constantine Cavafy puts it:

> Laistrygonians, Cyclops,
> wild Poseidon – you won't encounter them
> unless you bring them along inside your soul,
> unless your soul sets them up in front of you.

("Ithaka")

Blending the Joy and Practicality of Studying the Humanities

In fact, the *doesness* and *isness* of the humanities are inextricably intertwined.

Let us think about the role of the creative arts, a crucial component of the humanities. Even while teaching us, the arts insert a pause between the tick and the tock and in a sense suspend our diurnal lives. In defending the importance of the arts, perhaps we need to assert the value of that pause, whether it be attending a performance of a Balanchine ballet, a Mozart opera, a Beethoven symphony, or a blues concert by Buddy Guy. The joy and wonder evoked by such performances are real, if immeasurable, values.

By awakening our imagination, art intensifies and complements our own experience. Art represents people, cultures, values, and perspectives on living, but it does much more. While bringing us pleasure, art teaches us. While reading or contemplating a painting, our minds go elsewhere. We are taken on a journey into a world where form and meaning are intertwined.

Form matters. How a work of art is formally presented – its technique, its verbal or visual texture, its way of telling – gives pleasure. So does the inextricable relation between form and content. The form of imaginative art, as well as the form of well-written non-fiction, organizes the mess (if not the chaos) of personal life as well as that of external events. Form not only organizes and controls art but also other bodies of knowledge. Form gives structure that our own lives – as we move from moment to moment through time – may lack.

Narrative – sequential telling – imposes form as it orders and gives shape. Indeed, in the sense that each of us is continually giving shape to the stories we tell to and about ourselves, there is continuity between what we read and see and our own lives. Put another way, what we read teaches us to find narratives within our own lives and hence helps us make sense of who we are. Our seeing shapes and patterns in stories and other kinds of art helps give interpretive order – in the form of a narrative that we understand – to our lives. We live in our narratives, our discourse, about our actions, thoughts, and feelings.

While there is always a gulf between imagined worlds and real ones, does not the continuity between reading lives and reading texts depend on our understanding reading as a means of sharpening our perceptions and deepening our insights about ourselves? Reading is a process of cognition that depends on actively organizing the phenomena of language both in the moment of perception and in the fuller understanding that develops retrospectively.

Reading about the lives of others has practical value in organizing our own lives. I would also emphasize that how we extract and assimilate what we learn from the humanities into building our own lives varies from person to person, is not quantifiable, and is, in fact, an ongoing subject for cognitive studies.

In the aforementioned *New Yorker* article, Adam Gopnik takes a more reductive if sympathetic view of why people study the humanities, and in particular English:

> So why have English majors? Well, because many people like books. Most of those like to talk about them after they've read them, or while they're in the middle. Some people like to talk about them so much that they want to spend their lives talking about them to other people who like to listen. Some of us do this all summer on the beach, and others all winter in a classroom. One might call this a natural or inevitable consequence of literacy. And it's this living, irresistible, permanent interest in reading that supports English departments, and makes sense of English majors.

Teaching the Humanities

To cultivate both the utility of the humanities and their contribution to the quality of life, we need to develop passionate, committed teachers at every level whose knowledge, enthusiasm, and interest in students enable them to help open the doors and windows of students' minds to the importance of the humanities. Too often, university professors are so immersed in their own research that some courses offered are narrow in scope, inadequately defined, and unattractive to students.

Much more stress in college and university curricula should be placed on how to attract students rather than how to satisfy faculty. But that does not mean dummying down curricula by offering easy courses or by abandoning the canon of great (and sometimes) difficult works. Rather it means organizing the curricula so that the best teachers – those who truly engage students in the odyssey of learning – are foregrounded. Course syllabi must be more than maps of a teacher's taste and interest. They need to be an astute selection of texts as windows into cultural traditions and values. Teachers should remember that the goal of the humanities is not only to intensify and complement their students' life experiences, but also to give them tools to understand and interpret the world in which they live. This will help them be economically and professionally successful. Perhaps more importantly, the humanities will enhance their lives, enabling them to take pleasure in the arts and satisfaction in being part of an ongoing humanistic tradition of reading, writing, and thinking.

14

Do the Humanities Help Us Understand the World in Which We Live?

Introduction: How the Humanities Teach Us

What do the humanities do? I would argue that they help us understand ourselves and the world in which we live. When we read, we listen to words, respond to behavior, and try to judge what people's mindset is. We "read" human behavior every day in our interaction with colleagues, family, friends, and public figures, and our reading improves our knowledge, perspicacity, judgment, and sensitivity. In other words, reading helps us make sense of our lives and the world in which we live.

Reading literature and experiencing music, dance, live theater, and the visual arts are as much part of our life experience as other events and can have a similar impact. The humanities contribute to our moral, historical, and political awareness; this occurs even if the events described in a literary text, a painting or sculpture, or an operatic or theatrical performance are more imaginative than factually accurate.

Thus Joseph Conrad's *Heart of Darkness* (1898), with its stress on European imperial greed and racist exploitation of Africans, helps us understand the history of the country now called the Democratic Republic of Congo – formerly the Belgian Congo – and to some extent other former colonies in Africa. E.M. Forster's *A Passage to India* (1924) helps us understand India, particularly the continued divide between Muslims and Hindus and the more recent efforts in India to move beyond both its caste system and its colonial past with the goal of defining itself as an inclusive democracy.

How to Succeed in College and Beyond: The Art of Learning, First Edition. Daniel R. Schwarz.
© 2016 John Wiley & Sons, Ltd. Published 2016 by John Wiley & Sons, Ltd.

But let us turn to a current event, namely, Russian President Vladimir Putin's seizure of Crimea from Ukraine. What follows is not an apology for Putin's outrageous and duplicitous behavior but an effort to understand it through the lens of literature.

Putin, Dostoevsky, and Tolstoy as Examples of How We Learn and What We Learn from Literary Texts

Readers of Dostoevsky and Tolstoy will better understand Putin's behavior and his response to Western disapproval if they remember those nineteenth-century authors' deep skepticism regarding the Enlightenment's emphasis on logic and reason. Dostoevsky and Tolstoy believed in the Russian destiny and the exceptionalism of the Russian soul. While Putin shares many of their beliefs, we will also see that he ignores some of the humanistic implications of their fiction.

Although steeped in a Marxism that can be seen as a product of Enlightenment thinking, Putin sees himself as a Slavophil living by passion, faith, and intuition and unwilling to submit to Western views of reason and fairness. Reading Dostoevsky and Tolstoy, I believe, helps us understand Putin's disdain for the West. What Westerners may see as Putin's arrogant belief in Russian destiny needs to be understood in terms of a nation that fears not merely Western domination but Western invasion.

Putin's acute xenophobia mixed with suspicion of Western ways of thinking were on display when he announced plans to absorb Crimea into the Russian Federation:

> Some Western politicians are already threatening us not just with sanctions but also the prospect of increasingly serious problems on the domestic front. ... I would like to know what they have in mind exactly: action by a fifth column, this disparate bunch of "national traitors," or are they hoping to put us in a worsening social and economic situation so as to provoke public discontent?

According to David M. Herszenhorn, the author of "Xenophobic Chill Descends on Moscow," the April 2014 *New York Times* article from which the Putin quote came, Russia's "cultural policy emphasizes that 'Russia is not Europe' and urges 'a rejection of the principles of multiculturalism and tolerance' in favor of emphasizing Russia's 'unique state-government civilization.'" Among other things, Putin, when evoking multiculturalism and tolerance as Western ideas, is expressing his disdain for homosexuals.

Putin's mindset owes a good deal to Napoleon's and Hitler's invasions of Russia and the historical memory of those events. The Napoleonic invasion was never far from the nineteenth-century Russian imagination, and that is particularly true in Dostoevsky's and especially Tolstoy's case. Even more timely for Putin is the more recent invasion by Hitler in World War II; although the Russian President was born in 1952, the historical and personal memories of the horrors of World War II were a defining part of the world in which he grew up.

Putin believes that once again the West wants to shrink Russia – that is, the greater Russian empire he imagines – and that shrinkage has been going on since 1989. In his mind, the Russians lost no war but rather have been out-maneuvered to lose the peace. He detests any alliance between Ukraine and NATO. As the Russian state news network RT reported him saying on March 18, 2014: "NATO remains a military alliance, and we are against having a military alliance making itself at home right in our own backyard in our historic territory."

Putin claims to have read Tolstoy and Dostoevsky and includes the former's *Anna Karenina* and the latter's *Crime and Punishment* and *The Brothers Karamazov* among his favorite books (see the website Favobooks). Whether he reads them carefully or reads about them, he would have found in those authors strong evidence of national disunity, severe class division, decadence, alcoholism, and the need for transforming Russia by one means or another.

Dostoevsky cast his lot with the Slavophils, who were skeptical of Western ideas and thought Russia needed to maintain its cultural distinctiveness. That distinctiveness included spirituality and mysticism, as well as disdain for measuring and categorizing humans by scientific theories that fail to take account of each individual's uniqueness. In his introduction to Dostoevsky's *Notes from Underground* (1864), Robert G. Durgy contends:

> The Slavophils sought to dissociate Russia from the western influence and to discover her peculiarity in the old peasant commune that was believed to reveal her socialistic soul. Whereas the Westerners' doctrines were either frankly atheistic or at least areligious, the Slavophils believed in the primacy of the moral and religious laws of the Russian Orthodox Church and favored a holistic, spontaneous reason over the lower logical and analytic reason they associated with western positivism. (xi–xii)

Dostoevsky distrusted the abstract reasoning and logic that he believed dominated Western Europe and in particular the Enlightenment. That is, he thought that Russia must find its own way derived from its own past and cultural traditions.

He was doubtful that the light of reason could effectively enable humankind to illuminate, organize, and understand human behavior by means of social and scientific theories. Dostoevsky was skeptical of Western philosophical ideologies such as utilitarianism and political systems such as socialism or democracy that made rational claims about human behavior. He had great doubt that the scientific revolution would lead humankind to a better life or that humankind could step-by-step accumulate universal truths by evaluating hypotheses according to evidentiary tests. Nor did he believe we can predict behavior from observation as if a human being were an experiment within – to use a figure from *Notes from Underground* – a laboratory retort. Dostoevsky did not believe, as did some of his Russian contemporaries who bought into Social Darwinism, that humans were upwardly evolving and fulfilling a teleological pattern to a perfected or at least a much-improved humanity.

He thought that the only way for humankind to contain man's darker impulses – self-love, passions, desires, and impulses to narcissistic and destructive behavior – was through belief in God. Dostoevsky was something of a mystic who believed in the Russian soul inherent in each individual as well as a national collective entity accessible to all.

Dostoevsky understands that we humans do not always act logically and/or in our self-interest. With few exceptions, most notably Alyosha in *The Brothers Karamazov* (1880), Dostoevsky's characters not only lack modesty, balance, and gradualism but also at times respond to passions and needs that they barely understand or control.

In *Notes from Underground*, Dostoevsky is sympathetic to his narrator's rebellion against logic and reason and various Western social formulae, ranging from British utilitarianism (as defined by John Stuart Mill and Jeremy Bentham) with its concomitant Hedonic Calculus to the Romanticism of Rousseau with its idealization of human behavior. The Romantics believed humans were born with an inherent propensity toward the good and beautiful; were humans not corrupted by society, that natural propensity could be maintained.

Let us consider how Dostoevsky proposes an alternative to Western thought. For most of *Crime and Punishment* (1866) we are in the world of chronological, linear time where we hear the clock ticking and ask what will happen next. However, within the novel, there is another alternative reality and that is the one that matters most to Dostoevsky: the timeless reality of God and salvation. Believing in that reality creates the inner order, patience, and tranquility that define Sonya. This is the world of faith and the Bible, specifically the account of the resurrection of Lazarus which foreshadows Raskolnikov's transfiguration. Transfiguration takes place within significant time – what the Greeks called *kairos* – when the tick-tock of passing time doesn't matter. When Raskolnikov throws himself down at Sonya's feet in an act of humility, we are to understand that he experiences a transformation from immersion in the chronological world to awareness of this alternative, richer reality: "They were resurrected by love; the heart of each held infinite sources of life for the heart of the other" (Epilogue II, 549).

To some extent, Putin evokes both Dostoevsky's skepticism about Western reason and his mysticism. Although Putin's father was an atheist in keeping with Communist ideology, Putin was baptized into the Russian Orthodox Church under his mother's auspices. Since the 1990s he seems to have embraced Russian Orthodoxy; he makes clear that he wears a cross around his neck that was given to him by his mother. Whether he fervently believes or not, he wants the Russian people to see the cross as a link to the Slavophil tradition, just as he wants to advertise his supposedly remarkable physical fitness and outdoor adventures – including his claims of swimming in an extremely cold Siberian river and other derring-do – as alternatives to supposed Western decadence.

Let us turn to Tolstoy. Putin would certainly have found a source for Russian exceptionalism in Tolstoy's diagnosis of what was right and what was wrong with late nineteenth-century Russia. Tolstoy's focus in both *War and Peace* (1869) and *Anna Karenina* (1877) is Russia in the later nineteenth century after the freeing of the serfs in 1861 but still in the time of the Tsars. In the earlier novel, the focus is on the Napoleonic invasion and the perversion of Russian values by decadence that is often but not always of Western origin.

In *War and Peace*, Tolstoy's narrator is often a surrogate expressing the author's views: major events do not depend upon a hero's will but upon a confluence of causes. History is an accident informed by God's will which humans cannot understand; military action is more often farcical than the fulfillment of a plan. Humans need to isolate a comprehensible concatenation of events from the historical mess.

What makes life meaningful is human love, but finally we need to recognize God's miraculous world. We think we control far more in our personal lives than we do. Selfishness is bad and self-immersed narcissism is worse, but some self-love is necessary to act effectively. Tolstoy's conservative view of Russia's social structure sees the great families as necessary guardians of serfs and peasants.

In the combination of the characters' empty social prattle, family ambitions, and manipulative and self-serving discourse in *War and Peace*, Putin would have seen Russian decadence and examples similar to contemporary cocktail parties of influential people and wannabes. Even as the upper classes speak French, the gathering storm is Napoleon's expanding empire. Quite ironically, the first words we hear are Anna Pavlovna's French. As Count Rastopchin sarcastically remarks in 1811 when the restive Napoleon is proving an unreliable and patronizing ally: "[F]ar be it from us to fight the French. ... The French are our gods, and our kingdom of heaven is Paris" (2.5.iii.545).

Among the historical themes in both *War and Peace* and *Anna Karenina* that Putin takes from Tolstoy is the greatness and specialness of Mother Russia with its own Slavic traditions and culture, including its traditional rural communities as opposed to the impersonality and frivolity of the modern city and urban life. Notwithstanding his own luxurious lifestyle and his concept of "state capitalism," part of Putin's ideology is based on his appeal to the have-nots and to those who think traditional Communism was better. In *Anna Karenina*, he would have found underemployed and marginally employed workers whose safety is not taken seriously, as in the case of the railroad watchman accidentally killed when Anna meets Vronsky for the first time.

Putin claims to be concerned with how Russia is to organize itself morally and spiritually. In *Anna Karenina*, Konstantin Levin is a typifying character with historical resonance; he is struggling with the moral and economic issues facing large landowners once the serfs are freed. It is Levin's values that resonate with those of the other Tolstoy surrogate, the narrator. Tolstoy is scathingly critical of wasteful and dissolute ways of living by people of privilege. To an extent, Levin is the cultural answer to the triviality and superficiality of the world of Oblonsky, Vronsky, Anna, and her husband, Alexei Karenin.

Like his character Levin, Tolstoy believes that the Russian nobility have special responsibilities to the less fortunate, but he also believes that the Russian (Slavic) temperament and soul are different from those of Western Europeans. Levin's acceptance that he lives in a universe informed by God's presence transforms him into a fully functional person.

Many of Levin's – and Tolstoy's values – are implicit in Putin's espoused program. Like Tolstoy, Putin is impatient with the compromise and sluggishness of democracy, and he claims that his mission is to extend economic welfare to the less fortunate.

Putin's appeal is to Russian Manifest Destiny and the purity of the Russian land, now polluted in the Crimea and Eastern Ukraine. When we join Levin in the country in Part Two (Chapters xii–xvii; 151–73) of *War and Peace*, it is as if Tolstoy takes us into a different, cleaner, and clearer world than the urban world of Part One. Tolstoy's view of urban life, contemporary fashions, and political machinations is very much that of Levin. Tolstoy draws a strong contrast between what he sees as the superficiality of urban life and the substantive family-oriented life of those who live on the land. It is almost as if the Russian soil is a mystical presence shaping character. Yes, Tolstoy can be a polemicist – he hates triviality, licentiousness, and sloth – but he understands intuitively that human behavior cannot always be controlled by reason.

The question is whether Putin is misreading Dostoevsky and Tolstoy and doing so to cater to reductive and simplistic solutions that serve his own purposes. For there are also significant differences between Putin and both these authors, and, given the positivism of Marxist theory, which Putin still in large part embraces, we can see the irony of his invoking both of them. Moreover, while Tolstoy undermines the great man theory and sees much of history as accident, Putin sees himself as a larger-than-life figure unifying Russia in the wake of the terrible and catastrophic break-up of the USSR in 1991.

We might remember, when thinking about Putin's grandiose self-image, that Tolstoy detests Napoleon's megalomania, ambition, solipsism, and self-immersion. He presents Napoleon as a vain foolish man who is in over his head. He mocks Napoleon's invading Russia – he sarcastically calls him "that genius of geniuses" (4.2 viii.1001) — and thinks every major decision he made was wrong-headed. In *Christianity and Patriotism* (1896), Tolstoy wrote, "No feats of heroism are needed to achieve the greatest and most important changes in the existence of humanity."

Putin has done everything possible to remain close to the now independent nations that once composed the USSR. He plays on what he believes is the Russian desire for strong leadership, but Tolstoy was ironic about the transfiguring presence of a Tsar, and both Tolstoy and Dostoevsky were in fact far more concerned with spiritual values, the moral qualities of the individual, and the specialness of Russia under the auspices of God and less with power than the Machiavellian and xenophobic Putin, who often appeals in his intolerance to diversity — whether in his attitude toward sexual orientation or political opinions other than his own — to the lowest common denominator of the Russian sensibility. He may see himself as an heir to the Tsars and the charismatic Lenin and Stalin, but we see him as a deluded man following his passions. When it comes to Dostoevsky and Tolstoy, he is misreading the literary and historical analogies he invokes and ignores the essential humanism that shapes their view of personal relationships.

Conclusion

I conclude with an observation by Nicholas Kristof, in his April 16, 2015 piece "Starving for Wisdom," which emphasizes why we need the input of those who, unlike Putin, understand the humanities and read the great masterworks with tact and nuance:

> We need people conversant with the humanities to help reach wise public policy decisions, even about the sciences. Technology companies must constantly weigh ethical decisions: Where should Facebook set its privacy defaults, and should it tolerate glimpses of nudity? Should Twitter close accounts that seem sympathetic to terrorists? How should Google handle sex and violence, or defamatory articles?
>
> In the policy realm, one of the most important decisions we humans will have to make is whether to allow germline gene modification [see Nicholas Wade, "Scientists Seek Ban on Method of Editing the Human Genome"]. This might eliminate certain diseases, ease suffering, make our offspring smarter and more beautiful. But it would also change our species. It would enable the wealthy to concoct superchildren. It's exhilarating and terrifying. ...
>
> Even science depends upon the humanities to shape judgments about ethics, limits and values.

15

What to Do with a Bachelor of Arts in English

Introduction

I am often asked, "What can someone do with a BA in English?"

In 2012, I was giving a talk to an audience of over 100 at the midtown New York Public Library on my book *Endtimes? Crisis and Turmoil at the New York Times*. During the post-talk question period, someone who wandered in a few minutes before and was standing on the side – and apparently knew I was an English professor – asked somewhat aggressively; "And what do your students do?" Since I knew 15 or so of my former undergraduate students were in the audience, my response was: "Let's ask them." And as I went around the room, they responded: "I graduated from Harvard Law school and now work for the city of New York"; "I am at MoMA working on foundation relations after doing an MA in Museum Studies at NYU"; "I work at Christie's as a junior specialist in European furniture, porcelain, and decorative arts, after completing a Magister Literarum degree – accredited through the University of Glasgow – from Christie's Education"; "I am working in hospital administration"; "I work in the financial industry"; "I am preparing to take the law boards in a few months and am working as a paralegal"; "I am an editor in a major publishing house"; "I am a professor of English at a branch of CUNY"; "I am in medical school in New York," and so on.

Other former undergraduate majors whom I have taught have become authors and journalists (one, Eric Lichtblau of the *New York Times*, won a Pulitzer in 2006) or have been successful in the theater and film industries

How to Succeed in College and Beyond: The Art of Learning, First Edition. Daniel R. Schwarz.
© 2016 John Wiley & Sons, Ltd. Published 2016 by John Wiley & Sons, Ltd.

(I was Christopher Reeve's teacher and advisor). One is the founder of a major hedge fund.

Among those former English majors not in the audience, one writes for *Jane's*, which specializes in defense and military technologies; another wrote for *Brides* before going to law school; and a third works for an ad agency. Others do technical and business writing or are excelling in various areas of library administration.

English majors choose a major that not only challenges them intellectually but also gives them pleasure. They love to read and they think that reading matters. Or they hope to be writers and have taken courses in creative writing to test their potential as poets, fiction writers, and dramatists. They may have taken courses in expository writing to polish their skills or to see if the essay and other non-fictional forms are their best genres for a writing career.

English majors believe in education as an end, not merely as a stepping-stone on the path to a career, but they are not necessarily impractical. They are idealists, but unless they have large trust funds or expect an imminent inheritance or have immediate prospects for marrying into wealth, they need a career.

What English majors bring to career possibilities are the ability to think critically, speak articulately, write lucidly and precisely, and read powerfully, deftly, and with understanding of subtleties and nuances. They know how language works and have the written and oral skills to communicate effectively.

Possibilities

(1) English majors often go into teaching. In bygone years, we encouraged our best students to think about getting a Ph.D. and going into college teaching. Many of them did and had splendid careers. By encouraging hints, professors made me understand that I could get a Ph.D. and enter into the mysterious world of academics. It was almost like being tapped for a secret society.

In 2016, unless you really feel a calling akin to what I assume prospective clergy experience and are willing to teach anywhere in the country and perhaps at a small college with limited prestige or a two-year community college, you should think twice about graduate work. You can have a wonderful career teaching at such places, and you will find good students and colleagues everywhere. You may end up at a prestigious place, but job opportunities are more limited than they were when I went to grad school 50 years ago. If you do apply to graduate school in English, it is often better to wait a year after graduation so that if you graduate with honors or make Phi Beta Kappa, you have that on your application.

125

(2) Teaching secondary school is another option. Some Ph.D.s now teach at elite preparatory or public high schools, but the more traditional degree is a Masters degree in English, and if your choice is elementary school, a Masters in education. We used to say college teachers teach subject matter and high school teachers teach students. I like to think we teach subject matter to students. Teaching a subject at a top public school or private school can be challenging and exciting.

(3) Teach For America – a two-year commitment to teach at under-served schools – has become a program that many of our students seek out and find rewarding. Similar programs, such as New York's Urban Teaching Corps, also exist. This could lead to a career teaching students who are most in need, but it can also be a prelude to more traditional secondary teaching and/or public or private school administration.

(4) Teaching abroad is a possibility. A number of programs exist for placing students in English-speaking schools abroad and/or teaching English as a second language. The Peace Corps can be another teaching venue.

(5) A BA in English is often a prelude to law school. Doing well on LSATs will make an English major as competitive for law school as a major in any other field; reading deftly, writing precisely, thinking critically, and speaking well are important skills for a law career. I do need mention, however, that in recent years law school graduates are having a more difficult time finding career opportunities, and, as Elizabeth Olson has pointed out in the April 26, 2015 *New York Times*, some are saddled with enormous debts because of the large sums they borrowed to pay for law school.

(6) Some students pursuing medical and dental careers have double majors in English and biology or chemistry. A smaller number major only in English and take the essential science courses.

(7) Double majoring in English and economics is a good idea if you want to go into the business world, especially investment banking.

(8) English majors are often interested in becoming writers. Often the best way to pursue this is to get a MFA (Master of Fine Arts). The few years in a MFA program enable you to focus on writing and are also good prep-aration for a teaching position in a creative writing program, especially if your work is getting accepted by respectable publications.

(9) Many English majors become journalists. Several of my own Cornell students have done well in this field. Journalism has now expanded beyond print, radio, and TV broadcasting into the electronic media. In the past, a journalism degree was often a recommended path to a journalism career, but even more than in the past, journalism school is far from the only path. If you are interested in journalism, you need to get experience by writing for your college newspaper and doing summer internships in the media. Major papers sometimes hire students as part-time "stringers" who submit stories that pertain to their campus.

Unfortunately, some of the best internships do not pay. Recent litigation on the issue of unpaid interns may mean some of the media companies will cut down on such internships, but perhaps they will offer more paid ones. You may have a better chance of employment if you specialize in science writing, music reviews, etc., and have a weekly column or, even better, an editorship on the student newspaper.

Unless you are very well connected, your first journalism position will not be with prestige media like the *New York Times*, which tends to use other papers as a kind of farm system and to hire those writers whom they see as promising young stars. Smaller magazines and newspapers may pay less but will offer good opportunities for advancement.

(10) For those English majors considering publishing, summer internships are good because senior editors at publishing houses may get to see your work and observe how well you interact with a team. Once upon a time, publishing houses used to hire women as typists and fact checkers even if they had outstanding academic records, but now publishers are for the most part equal opportunity employers.

(11) Needing writers for publicity and for publishing reports to stockholders and clients, businesses hire English majors. So do ad agencies, which need clever writers. Non-profit organizations need people who write well. Politicians and some CEOs need speechwriters. English majors are also hired by major investment banking firms because the firms see the potential to develop capable young adults who are imaginative, innovative, and have communication and people skills. Again, summer internships can open the door to being hired for long-term positions.

To quote again from Nicholas Kristof's "Starving for Wisdom," "[L]iberal arts equip students with communications and interpersonal skills that are valuable and genuinely rewarded in the labor force, especially when accompanied by technical abilities." He cites Harvard Labor economist Lawrence Katz: "A broad liberal arts education is a key pathway to success in the 21st-century economy." Kristof goes on to summarize Katz: "The economic return to pure technical skills has flattened, and the highest return now goes to those who combine soft skills – excellence at communicating and working with people – with technical skills."

127

Interviews

When you go to interviews, even med school interviews, you will be asked why you majored in English. Think of something to say beforehand such as – and these are only suggestions – "I majored in English because reading about other cultures and time periods complemented my life experience" or "No other major would have taught me so much about how people behave in various circumstances and in various cultures. More than any other major I might have chosen, the English major helped me learn how other people live, what values motivate them, and why and how people think and feel."

Among qualities to stress in an interview: you write lucidly; you know how to organize and synthesize complex material; you are an experienced researcher, comfortable with the Internet and libraries; and you are a savvy member of the twenty-first-century digital universe. Furthermore, you not only speak articulately and confidently, but you also have made effective presentations to audiences.

Emphasize that, having taken small classes and seminars, you know how to work within a community: you have exceptional listening skills, work well with peers and supervisors, and learn from others.

Keep in mind that you want to be offered a position not for what you are but for what you will become. That is, you want to be hired not only for the posted entry-level job but also for your potential for growth. You should emphasize that you want to be an important asset and will take initiatives within assigned tasks.

Keep a notebook for possible answers to expected questions. Whether it be a job or university interview, always go to interviews informed about the place interviewing you. Foreground what makes you the very person the inter-viewers want.

Always dress appropriately. Be neat but not flamboyant. What might be appropriate for a major company in the financial industry might not be best for Teach For America, where expensive clothes might have the interviewer won-dering how you are going to be able to teach in the South Bronx or on an Indian reservation.

Conclusion

I asked a few of my former students how they use their English major. Kayla Rakowski Dryden, Cornell '08, whose title at MoMA is Development Officer, Foundation Relations, observed:

I use the writing and proofreading skills I honed as an English major every single day, whether I am drafting a grant proposal, editing down content for a donor report, or simply typing emails and business correspondence. Further, the major greatly expanded my knowledge of cultural history, building a context that is a great asset to me as an employee of an art museum.

Devon Goodrich, Cornell '07, Harvard Law '11, Assistant Corporation Counsel in the Environmental Law Division of New York City, noted:

[T]he reading comprehension and writing skills that I developed as an English major gave me an edge over other law students and young lawyers. ... [T]he ability to closely read a text while also placing the text within its larger context directly translates to law. Practicing law involves reading all aspects of a situation – not only the applicable statutes or regulations, but also the clashing personalities of involved parties, the historical background of a project or property, and the political circumstances surrounding a case – and providing sound advice based on all the facts and angles. ... Often when reading a legal document, the best readers can read what is not said in the document as well as the words on the page.

Playwright and actress Zoe Geltman, Cornell '08, observed: "Majoring in English has definitely contributed to my appreciation of the arts and of litera-ture in general. I think it has made me a more thoughtful, insightful person and made it easy and natural for me to analyze a piece of text – be it a play, a piece of fiction, or an article." Liz Wight, Cornell '07, added: "I think the thing the major gave me most was critical thinking, a yearning for discovery and clear means of articulating myself."

Sal Ruggiero, Cornell '07, who has been an Editor and is now Assistant Manager, Domestic Rights for the Knopf Doubleday Publishing Group, eloquently explained: "Reading and writing not just well but for a purpose has proved paramount to my job. ... Plus learning argument and persuasion techniques in essay writing sometimes proves useful in contract negotiation or pitching." Amanda First, Cornell '12, former Assistant Editor at *Brides*, put it: "My English major has lent me creative, critical thinking and analytic writing skills that have made my writing clearer, more exciting, and more serviceable to our readers."

Grace Jean, Cornell 2000, a US naval reporter who writes for *Jane's* as well as a part-time music reviewer for the *Washington Post*, brings the commentary from my former students to an apt conclusion:

All the skills that I developed and honed through my English classes and seminars are put to use daily in my career as a journalist. Close reading, analytical thinking, and clear and concise writing have become the bread and butter of my livelihood. I have the English major to thank for playing an integral role in my professional development.

Lest it be thought my students represent the elite segment of college graduates, I quote Lyndsay Hines, Southwestern Oklahoma State University '15 and currently an English teacher in Taloga, Oklahoma:

> [As English majors] we are taught structure and discipline through the rules and logic of grammar and linguistics. At the same time, we are taught to analyze a world of literature that, in some instances, does not follow the rules of logic or grammar. We are often expected to use deep thinking and personal reasoning skills. Finally, we are given a creative outlet through reading and writing. The uses of this in the classroom, I have found, are endless.

What all these comments show is that the English major opens doors through which students walk to a splendid and varied future.

16

Does It Make Sense to Pursue a Humanities Doctorate? The Pros and Cons of Graduate Education in the Humanities

Introduction

You loved studying literature in college and thought how much fun it would be to become a professor leading the discussions you enjoyed. What if you could turn your love of reading and thinking about what you read into a lifetime career? Maybe even write a novel or poems? Spend your days on a beautiful campus?

These dreams were my dreams and for the most part college teaching fulfilled them, but is that opportunity still available in the first quarter of the twenty-first century?

What you need to know before deciding to pursue a Ph.D. in the humanities is that when you finish your degree you will be entering a very difficult job market, in part because many colleges and universities supplement their tenured faculty with adjuncts. Former Chair of the Berkeley English Department Sam Otter observes: "I only suggest graduate school to the very best undergraduates I teach. The employment situation seems more dire than I ever have seen it, with little prospect for improvement."

Even if you do get a position at an elite college, it may be only after some combination of postdocs, teaching off the tenure track, and/or holding a tenure track position at a college that is not the prestigious school of your dreams.

How to Succeed in College and Beyond: The Art of Learning, First Edition. Daniel R. Schwarz.
© 2016 John Wiley & Sons, Ltd. Published 2016 by John Wiley & Sons, Ltd.

Young faculty are often getting tenure at Cornell 10 years later than I did because they had post-docs and positions that did not offer tenure or they began teaching elsewhere.

The job market becomes even more difficult if your personal circumstances – say, a partner whose work is in a specific place – constrain you from looking throughout the US and perhaps even abroad. Subtracting yourself from all but one geographic area makes the job search all that much more difficult.

You will have a better chance if you are also open to community college teaching or secondary school teaching, perhaps at a strong private school or even a first-rate public school. Clearly it will be more difficult to do research or write that novel or play in positions where you are teaching a much heavier load, but it is not impossible and has often been done.

How to Proceed If You Are Sure Graduate School Is for You

Often a gap year is a good strategy. If you make Phi Beta Kappa as a senior and graduate with honors, you will be a more attractive candidate when applying for admission during the year after your senior year compared to applying in the middle of your senior year. Furthermore, you will have time to study for the GRE exams that many top schools require.

Be sure the people who write your recommendations are enthusiastic about you. Also, be sure they are reliable since, alas, some professors do not do this task in a timely and conscientious manner. If a professor comes to class prepared, meets office hours on time, returns essays with alacrity, and shows interest in his or her students – and particularly in you – you will have an idea how reliable and interested that faculty member is in writing your recommendations. Since the genre requires some hyperbole, it is good to choose people who know how to write recommendations.

Getting a Masters degree first can be a good idea, for two main reasons: you can see if grad school is for you, and you can prepare to apply to a more prestigious school if you are not admitted where you wished. But be aware that if you begin your doctorate at a different school, you probably will lose time. That is, students entering with a Masters degree do not finish two years sooner and often do not finish even one year before students who began right after taking their BA.

Apply widely to graduate schools and choose some that are not in the first tier and a few that are safety schools. You can always decide not to go to the latter, but in my experience those who apply only to elite schools and don't get in – even if they know this might happen – are devastated. If your finances are tight, most schools will waive the application fee. Although the job market is discouraging, applicant numbers are still very high, and many of the elite schools, in recognition of the difficult job market situation, are taking fewer students than they once did.

While you apply to universities, admission and fellowship decisions are made by the department in which you wish to study. Your application should show that you know something about the department faculty and programs to which you are applying. This means that you will need to fine-tune each application so that it reveals a personal awareness of and interest in all the departments to which you are applying.

You do need to study for the GRE exams. One way to study is to read the Norton Anthologies of British and American Literature. How well you do will make a difference, particularly in this era of grade inflation where most applicants have close to the same grades. Some schools take the subject exam (in the case of applicants to English departments, "Literature in English") more seriously than others, but in my experience, the major stress is on the candidate's Verbal and Analytic Writing scores.

Corresponding with professors with whom you might study may be helpful to your application, but be aware that only a small number of professors serve on the graduate admissions committee each year and they are the ones who, for the most part, have the final say. Also be aware that admission is quite subjective. On virtually every selection committee I have ever been on, I can say that if one person in the room were different, the outcome would be different because the dynamic among those making these decisions would be changed.

Two big variables are who is on the committee and what their inclinations are. I have been on committees where foreign language facility mattered a great deal to one member, and I admit to thinking myself that if one cannot do reasonably well on the quantitative GRE, the student may not have the best reasoning power.

What the foregoing means is that you will probably be admitted to some programs and not to others, and you may be offered a more generous aid package by one school than by others. If the more generous offer is not from the most prestigious school that admits you, you will have a difficult decision. Sometimes, you can tell a school you have had a better offer and that school might come up with a bit more money.

If you are thinking of an MFA, you should know that the numbers of applicants are even higher at top programs than for Ph.D. programs. For the 2015–16 entering class, the Cornell English Department extended admission offers to 22 Ph.D. students and one joint MFA/Ph.D. student out of 258 applicants. The MFA program extended offers to eight students out of 810 applicants, less than one in a hundred.

What the MFA does is give you a chance to write; at Cornell, it is a two-year degree with an additional two years as a teaching assistant. But you need to know that unless you are recognized as an important talent on the basis of already published material, your getting a position at the conclusion of an MFA is even more difficult than at the conclusion of a Ph.D. program.

After admission to a graduate program, prospective graduate campus visits are much more valuable than undergraduate ones. If you are admitted to a number of schools, you might want to visit the ones that you are most likely to attend and to speak to the professors with whom you might study and with the students who are in the program. If professors seem uninterested in you and morale among students is not high, you might think of going elsewhere, providing you have that choice.

What Students Need to Know

Be aware that you will be investing five or six years of life in a process that may not yield a place in the college teaching profession and that a job in a major research university is even less likely. Those who do get such jobs often begin elsewhere and get noticed by writing important articles and books. Graduate students in the humanities are usually those who loved learning as undergraduates, but – and these categories are not mutually exclusive – they may also be people who didn't know what else to do.

Many grad students convince themselves that the joy of learning is enough, but when they don't get positions, they are heart-broken. Students may convince themselves that jobs don't matter when they are accepted in graduate school at 22 or 23, especially if they have a five-year support package, but they are often devastated when they can't find a position at 29.

If your goal is to be a professor, you need to be aware that colleges and universities tend to hire from the top graduate schools, and this is even more true of the elite schools (see Joel Warner and Aaron Clauset, "The Academy's Dirty Secret").

On the other hand, in my experience, some community colleges and smaller colleges and satellite regional campuses of some state universities are more likely to hire those with strong teaching credentials who may not have Ph.D.s from elite research universities.

Crucial Decision: Choosing a Graduate Mentor and a Graduate Committee

In most doctoral programs, you have a graduate committee composed of three or four members. I actually prefer three because it is less cumbersome to get people together and functioning as a team. An alternative is to have three but have an informal fourth who reads dissertation chapters and gives advice when needed.

Whom you choose as chair of that committee is essential, even though the other committee members should also be mentors. In general you should choose faculty with whom you have taken classes and received positive feedback. Each member should represent a somewhat different field. One way of preparing yourself for the job market is to have range: small colleges are looking for people to cover their curriculum rather than research scholars who can teach graduate seminars in your dissertation subject.

As much as you want a match for your specific interest, I would recommend that, wherever you go, you should seek mentors who are fully interested in you and your progress. I never felt that I was any better a mentor for those working in my exact areas of interest than for those whose work was close enough to mine so I could helpful.

When choosing your graduate committee chair, you need to keep in mind three rules:

(1) You should choose a mentor who is interested in you as well as his/her subject and one who knows the difference between mentoring and creating a clone. The best mentoring is helping a student find his or her own way.

(2) You should choose a mentor who thinks of mentoring as an essential part of his or her professional responsibility and who is not only there for you whenever needed while you are a graduate student but who also understands that mentoring does not stop with the awarding of a Ph.D. You want someone to whom you can always turn at every stage of your career for advice and timely recommendations. Be aware that professors who have trouble giving back papers and chapters within a week or so will be equally unreliable when you need them for other things later.

(3) In general, choose someone who answers emails promptly, keeps office hours, and also has reasonable social skills. It is not easy to deal with eccentrics, and there are many in academia. Ideally, you want someone who is a good listener, advocates for you when necessary, and is enthusiastic about both his or her teaching and his or her research.

Necessary Skills

The most important skills for graduate success are similar to those for undergraduates: time management (knowing where your time goes each day) is essential. Moreover, you must know the program's requirements – including whatever qualification exams precede thesis writing – and you need to make a schedule with your graduate committee to meet them. You need to be proactive in discussing these requirements with your committee because they may be inattentive to moving you forward.

Begin projects when they are assigned, leave time for drafts, understand expectations, and participate in seminars. Make sure you take time every day to do something that is fun, whether that means going to the gym, practicing the guitar, or taking a walk. Take time to make friends at your new school.

First-year graduate students often have a little trouble adjusting to their programs. They have been validated stars in their undergraduate programs but now they are in some sense beginning students in a program where the older students are the stars. Sometimes, especially in the first term, first-year graduate students feel like freshmen. If they come from less prestigious schools, they may also worry about whether they can compete with students from an elite school. Keep in mind that you were selected in a rigorous selection process because the department committee thinks you can do the work.

It is up to the graduate program to help in the transition, but you should be aware that feelings of inadequacy and self-doubt are almost universal. If you are having problems, speak to the Graduate Field Representative or, better yet, a professor with whom you are taking a seminar. Be aware, too, of the mental health facilities on campus, and use them if necessary.

The Doctoral Program's Responsibility

Training college teachers should be an important focus since teaching college is the position most grad students want. At Cornell we have an excellent freshman writing program, and graduate students in several humanities fields spend the summer between their first and second year as apprentice teachers. In their second year, they usually teach their own class under the supervision of a course director. While commendable, this still leaves us with inexperienced teachers. To some extent we pretend that teaching is better than it is and that one summer of training makes a master teacher.

Mentoring teaching should continue throughout the graduate career, but this responsibility is not always fulfilled in doctoral programs, despite the fact that most of our graduate students aspire to be professors. Every doctoral committee should have a teaching mentor who visits the graduate students' classes and meets one-on-one with the graduate student to discuss what has been observed. The mentor and student should be having a continuing dialogue on teaching methods throughout his or her graduate career. Needless to say, the mentor must be a skilled teacher. Ideally, funding would be available to enable the student to work with the mentor as a teaching assistant not only in large lecture classes but also in smaller classes.

Programs that put skilled teachers on the market will have a placement advantage, especially at small liberal arts colleges. The emphasis on quality teaching at research universities has improved and has always been important in English departments. Thus research universities will be looking for those who will be able to teach undergraduates as well as to give specialized seminars and mentor graduate students. Certainly, the chances of getting a position at a small liberal arts college, a community college, a regional campus of a major state university, or even a secondary school are increased by having had mentored and supervised teaching experience.

Moving Forward or Taking Time to Build Credentials?

Let me segue to a complicated topic: the current length of graduate school in the humanities and whether it is necessary. Given the lack of jobs, should graduate programs be speeding up the process rather than slowing it down? We are dealing often with adults in their mid to late twenties and it can be demeaning and can lead to arrested development if they remain students for six or seven years prior to seeking employment. If they are going to get a position after years of trying, do we want them to be well into their thirties?

Now, because students need publications and conferences, they often take longer than five years to complete their degree, but perhaps we should streamline that process. Too many graduate students take weeks off preparing a conference paper for a tiny audience or belong to several time-consuming reading groups. On the other hand, as my Cornell colleague Greg Londe contends, if one chooses to give conference papers that lead to dissertation progress, they may serve a useful purpose. Perhaps a balanced approach is to recommend, prior to entering the job market, a few conference papers within five years but also stress the importance of getting one or more of those conference papers published.

I believe that we need to figure out a program that lasts five years, including teaching assistant years and a fellowship year. Admission to candidacy exams should take place no later than the sixth term. We should encourage students to find a dissertation topic or at least focus on a research area as early as possible, and encourage course essays that become early versions of dissertation chapters. Sometimes faculty are dilatory in grading papers, encourage Incompletes by raising the bar unreasonably high for course papers when they should consider course essays as necessary exercises, and fail to push students to take exams and submit chapters.

Career Preparation

We need, as I have been stressing, to make clear that many if not most Ph.D. students are not going to get tenure-track jobs at research institutions and that many of those getting jobs will be teaching heavy loads at small and not elite liberal arts colleges and community colleges. We need to warn them about a system that can exploit them by offering low-paying adjunct jobs.

I recommend that graduate programs in the humanities have an informal continuing colloquium for students about alternative careers to academic teaching/research positions. Such a colloquium should be a component of Ph. D. programs in the humanities.

We need to present other opportunities for graduate students in the humanities, including positions in non-profit charitable foundations that support educational initiatives as well as positions in student services, cultural institutions (especially museums which publish catalogues and also require research and writing skills for their exhibits), journalism, publishing, and the new media.

Perhaps, as we open more doors to what Ph.D.s might do, we should consider whether we can train them to write for a larger audience as serious journalists or staff writers for major and influential magazines or as freelance writers. We might invite non-fiction writers to give colloquiums or even teach courses as well as suggest that graduate students enroll in journalism classes on campuses that have them?

Part of the problem is educating our colleagues, who need to be aware of these other career paths as they prepare and advise graduate students. Many are so deeply immersed in their own narrow research and in academic politics that they have a limited perspective on other opportunities.

In some fields, people with doctorates can move back and forth between industry and academia. Celebrity public figures and some creative writers have been able to do this, but it is rare in the humanities. In STEM areas, however, there are many more opportunities for positions in private industry, especially in fields like pharmaceuticals and computer engineering where research is paramount and publication encouraged.

Literary Scholars as Public Intellectuals

We humanists need to speak to those outside the academy and strive to be public intellectuals bridging, by means of ideas and lucid prose, the gap between academia and those in the larger community who are interested in the various arts. We need to address those making political and economic decisions that have an impact on public life, including on cultural institutions and universities. We need to think of our graduate students of today as potentially the public intellectuals of tomorrow. We need to teach graduate students to write for a broader audience so that they will bridge the gap between scholars and those in the public who are readers and thinkers as well as those who are members of influential political and cultural communities.

I applaud Kevin Birmingham's effort in *The Most Dangerous Book: The Battle for James Joyce's Ulysses* to write for a larger audience rather than to join those academic ostriches who pretend there is no audience beyond specialists. I also applaud his Harvard mentors, at least one of whom, Louis Menand, plays a role in public discourse. To shift metaphors, Birmingham eschews academic mole work that makes readers think: "Something must be going on down there because of the small pile of dirt next to the holes, but what exactly it is we cannot ascertain." Indeed, much of my considerable enthusiasm for Birmingham's project derives from his efforts to write as a literary intellectual reaching out to an audience that goes beyond Joyce scholars.

We need to eschew jargon that interferes with communication, and we need to be wary about assuming that we are moving teleologically forward in criticism and scholarship, an assumption that leads to patronizing past scholarly approaches. Chances of placement outside academia increase when one can write lucid precise prose without reveling in specialized academic-speak.

Conclusion

After reading the foregoing, James Phelan, Distinguished University Professor at Ohio State, advised:

> I would recommend ... say[ing] even more explicitly "don't go with the expectation that you'll get a tenure-track job." Instead, "go with your eyes open that the likelihood of getting a tenure-track job is very small and thus that you'll be doing something else with your Ph.D. than college teaching for a decent wage." In other words, "go because you want to spend the next five years of your life studying this field before you move on to something else. Ask yourself hard questions: Do you want to spend five years with wages not that far above the poverty line? Are you likely to look back and regret spending this time being trained for a profession that you're not going to enter?" Then say, "If you still want to go, here's my advice."

I have tried to balance hard realism with at least a little optimism since some people do get good positions even if the overwhelming majority do not.

For me, the academic life – teaching bright and committed students – and writing about literature and culture has been a perfect fit. But I am hesitant to advise you to pursue an academic career in view of the job market. With financial exigencies caused in part by a decline in state aid for public universities and in part by rising expenses, some of which are mandated by laws, as well as a decline in humanities majors, I cannot foresee that the job market will improve. Add to this the often exploitive hiring of underpaid adjuncts and you see the reason for my hesitation.

For one thing, there are too many already-minted Ph.D.s hoping to get the opportunity to occupy a tenure-track line. For another, starting a tenured job in your later thirties after post-docs and short-term lectureships or non-tenured assistant professorships limits your career development compared with those professors in the past who had tenure-track jobs 10 years sooner. I see people getting tenure in their mid-forties, which delays having children and some of the other pleasures of an economically and socially stable adulthood.

Nevertheless, if you are willing to immerse yourself in your studies with the knowledge that the future is indeterminate, and you have the good fortune to get full support from a strong department, I would still caution you about the odds of getting an academic position, but I would not discourage you from trying.

Part V

Perspectives of a Professor

17

Are Teaching and Research Mutually Exclusive?

I say research and teaching are … inseparable. And they are symbiotic.
(Cornell Nobel Laureate Roald Hoffmann)

After Adam Grant proposed in a February 5, 2014 *New York Times* article that tenure should be awarded for good teaching as well as good research, I thought about his claim that research showed that, "In all fields and all kinds of colleges, there was little connection between research productivity and teaching ratings by students and peers."

Saul Teukolsky, Cornell's Hans A. Bethe Professor of Astronomy and Physics, observes:

> The study he cites basically lumps together many levels of teaching in many kinds of institutions (not restricted to research universities) and finds little connection between teaching and research. No surprise: You don't have to be a strong researcher to do a good job of teaching freshman calculus or freshman composition. Since most university teaching is at the freshman level, this is the effect the study finds. But in my experience the strongest teachers of upper-level undergrad courses and graduate courses tend to be the strongest researchers. Of course there are exceptions, but statistically I believe this is true.

I am not a social scientist and am basing what follows on my almost five decades of college teaching in the humanities, mostly at Cornell but with a few visiting professorships at state universities. I have been fortunate to have won Cornell's major teaching awards and have had some success as a scholar.

How to Succeed in College and Beyond: The Art of Learning, First Edition. Daniel R. Schwarz.
© 2016 John Wiley & Sons, Ltd. Published 2016 by John Wiley & Sons, Ltd.

The connection between teaching and research depends on a number of variables, including where one teaches, how many courses one teaches, what the teaching expectations are, what field one teaches in, and what kind of students one teaches. It also depends on the criteria by which one rates teachers. But what is clear is that those who do research find a strong relationship between their teaching and research, and in most cases that teaching includes undergraduate teaching. As observed by Ron Ehrenberg, Cornell's Irving M. Ives Professor of Industrial and Labor Relations and Economics and an authority on higher education: "Put simply, my research enhances my undergrad teaching and my undergrad teaching enhances my research."

In my experience, teaching has become foregrounded in STEM courses. Or as Associate Professor David Delchamps, Cornell Electrical and Computer Engineering, notes: "We have to regard teaching as a mission we'd like to accomplish optimally rather than a burden we need to share equitably."

My own experience as a teacher-scholar in the humanities makes me skeptical of the claim that there is no relation between effective teaching and effective research. Beth Newman, Associate Professor of English and Director of Women's and Gender Studies at Southern Methodist University, observes:

> We do not produce tangible or marketable goods but knowledge. And that knowledge must not be confused with *information*. It is more often interpretation, in its broadest sense of re-framing of other knowledge for new social and cultural contexts. It is difficult to invest intellectually in this knowledge and to keep current in it, and therefore, to teach it responsibly to others, if one is not also producing it at some level.

It has been my impression that at Cornell and peer institutions, the most esteemed and productive scholars in the humanities have been for decades the most effective teachers, especially for the best students. But I decided to ask a number of colleagues in diverse fields – humanists, social scientists, and scientists – what they thought about the relationship between their own teaching and research. Virtually all of them expressed the view that their teaching and research were strongly interrelated.

For me, there has always been a strong correlation between my teaching and writing. In a classroom, one learns to organize material, articulate it lucidly and precisely, and defend one's ideas, and that is also what one does when presenting research. To be sure, I have given many presentations based on my research at academic conferences and in other venues, but the often small audiences at conferences do not always test you as much as a bright and informed group of graduate students or advanced undergraduates. Thus teacher-scholars in the humanities often test their hypotheses in the classroom before bringing them to conferences or submitting them to journals.

I am fortunate to teach in the humanities at a university where I have time to do research and where there is a strong relationship between what I study and what I teach. Indeed much of my scholarship derives from my teaching experience. Right now, I am working on a book on the European novel since 1900 that will include a chapter on Proust's *Swann's Way*. My reading and thinking about Proust informs what I bring not only to my graduate seminar on the Modern Imagination but also to my graduate and undergraduate seminars on Joyce's *Ulysses* in terms of narrative theory, and the experience of testing my ideas has helped my understanding of Proust's narrative strategies.

Most of Cornell's best scholars in diverse fields believe that teaching helps their research. Nobel Laureate in Chemistry and Frank H.T. Rhodes Professor of Humane Letters emeritus, Roald Hoffmann writes: "I have thought about [the relation between teaching and research] over the years, and overall reached the conclusion that it works in both directions, and importantly for me, teaching introductory chemistry has made me a better researcher." Cornell Professor of Mathematics Louis Billera writes compellingly about how even properly taught introductory classes are informed by the need to explain how specific material fits into the context of a larger field:

Early on, I noticed that my research benefited each time I taught a course I hadn't taught before. Organizing a subject in order to teach it, especially to undergraduates, meant you had to really know it, not just have what we call "a nodding acquaintance" with the material (which means you can nod sagely when hearing a colloquium lecture about it). Conversely, I think it is important to know where a subject is going as well as where it has been to be a truly effective teacher. Those not involved in research tend not to know much, if anything, about the former. Where a subject is going, which includes how it might be used, is essential to get and keep student attention, again, especially that of undergraduates.

What follows is not, I hope, a boastogram, but an informal account of my own experience. Had I not taught James Joyce's *Ulysses* many times and worked through my approach in a classroom, I would not have been able to write *Reading Joyce's Ulysses*. Following my mantra, "Always the text; always historicize," while teaching other modern writers – including Joseph Conrad, Wallace Stevens, D.H. Lawrence, T.S. Eliot, Virginia Woolf, and E.M. Forster – certainly helped in writing chapters and books about them. Doing research – learning about these writers' historical contexts, their lives, and the ways they have chosen to transform their experience and imagination into literary form – immeasurably helped my teaching. Much of my literary and cultural research has been shaped by the interaction of studying the aforementioned authors' work and my presenting what I have discovered to both graduate and undergraduate students.

Indeed, one of the joys of teaching is learning something new every day both in the preparation of classes and in the insightful responses of students.

Years ago during the high tide of Deconstruction, I wrote an influential book (*The Humanistic Heritage: Critical Theories of the English Novel from James to Hillis Miller*) on the history and practice of the Anglo-American literary method and theory as it pertained to fiction. I refined the ideas for the book not only in upper class and graduate classes but also in an informal colloquium attended by graduate students with whom I was working and by any other graduate student who wanted to come. Directing several Summer Seminars for College Teachers for the NEH (National Endowment for the Humanities) gave me the chance to present the ideas for the aforementioned book. Later, teaching NEH Summer Seminars contributed to the book I wrote in the 1990s about the relationship between modern art and modern literature.

When I write for a professional audience or for readers outside the academy, I write as a teacher imagining my audience as those interested in knowing what I have learned. What effective teachers and good scholars have in common is a joy in the process of learning and of sharing what they have learned with others.

My Cornell colleague George Hutchinson, Newton C. Farr Professor of American Culture, observes: "My book on the Harlem Renaissance resulted from teaching African American literature surveys on the one hand and advanced courses on Whitman and the American Renaissance on the other. I wanted to see how these fields intersected and it resulted in that book." He adds:

> Every time I teach a course, I teach some stuff I've never taught or even read before, and in the process of preparing to teach it and then actually teaching it, I do research, take notes, perform in class, and then take stock of where I've ended up. Even if I never end up writing an article about the new text I've just taught, I learn a lot from teaching it and it adds to my knowledge of the fields in which I am engaged.

Research has also driven my own syllabi. As soon as Imre Kertész won the Nobel Prize in Literature, I put *Fatelessnesss* on my syllabus for my "Imagining the Holocaust" seminar, even though I had not yet read it. If my past work and book on Holocaust memoirs, diaries, novels, and films helped me interpret *Fatelessnes,* teaching it brought me new insights. As I learned more about Woolf, Forster, and Wilde for my books on Modernism, my syllabus for my lecture class on twentieth century British literature changed. A handful of years ago I was invited on the 150th anniversary of *On the Origin of Species* to give a public lecture on Darwin and modern literature, and realized that much of what I thought I knew about Darwin's theory of evolution was out of date.

Researching that lecture improved the accuracy of my presentation of intellectual and cultural history in the same twentieth century British literature course.

Curiosity, the desire to share knowledge, and enthusiasm for watching young adults develop their potential are essential to effective teaching at the college level. Similar qualities drive research. Good scholars must find ways to convince other scholars that their scholarship matters and that their findings are to be taken seriously; their presentation of research is a kind of teaching. Indeed, as Nicholas Kristof has argued in his 2014 *New York Times* column, "Professors, We Need You!," for researchers to reach out to larger audiences and be public intellectuals, they must be lucid writers and not simply produce dry scholarship dressed up in incomprehensible jargon.

I have always been skeptical about a scholar from another field who can't tell me in layman's terms what he or she is doing. If the scholar's explanation is so abstruse, how is that person going to teach undergraduates – or even graduates – to say nothing of freshmen?

Often the best teachers leave a mark that lasts for decades, sometimes in ways that can't be quantified, such as arousing an interest in literature, art, and music that grows into a passion or arousing a desire to find scientific and technological answers to significant problems and perhaps contribute to solving issues that sustain life. Truly inspiring teachers – who, among other wonderful results, often teach students to become teacher-scholars – are unforgettable and accompany us throughout our lives.

18

The Classroom as Opportunity: Teaching Students How to Enjoy and Understand Literature, Read Closely, Write Lucidly, and Think Independently

I am more optimistic about what happens at Ivy League and elite universities than William Deresiewicz, who has complained about students at so-called elite colleges who lack creativity and whose main concern is career success:

> [W]e have constructed an educational system that produces highly intelligent, accomplished twenty-two-year-olds who have no idea what they want to do with their lives; no sense of purpose and, what is worse, no understanding of how to go about finding one. Who can follow an existing path but don't have the imagination – or the courage, or the inner freedom – to invent their own. (*Excellent Sheep*, 25)

My experience is quite different from his. As I have indicated before, I have been teaching at Cornell as an English professor since 1968, with occasional forays into different fields and visiting professorships elsewhere. I find that most of my students take joy in learning. I see students enthusiastically learning for the sake of learning, thinking critically, developing their potential, expanding their interests, and growing a great deal in their undergraduate years. Every day I see innovative minds thinking seriously, imaginatively, and often originally about the ideas and experiences that they confront. They volunteer not so much

How to Succeed in College and Beyond: The Art of Learning, First Edition. Daniel R. Schwarz.
© 2016 John Wiley & Sons, Ltd. Published 2016 by John Wiley & Sons, Ltd.

to build their CVs, but because they care and want to make important contributions to build a better world in science, government, journalism, and teaching as well as many other fields.

The best teachers are interested in education as both a means and an end. While most students are motivated by career aspirations, they also have a strong idealistic desire to learn about themselves and the world in which they live. Those in STEM programs and the social sciences are often no less engaged in the poetry and joy of learning than those in the humanities. This is particularly true of those with a theoretical bent.

Most Cornell students do develop wide interests and discover the joy of learning, although of course the degree of exploration in fields outside their own and the quality of their innovative thinking vary. As an English professor, I am struck by how many students, including those in STEM programs, want to explore history, literature, art, and music as part of their learning process, and by how many of the humanities students have an interest in basic science. A great deal of exploration takes place in extra-curricular activities such as participating in college publications, playing in the orchestra, and acting in plays.

To be sure, there have been radical changes not only in what my colleagues and I teach, but also in how students learn. The digital world has changed learning in two fundamental ways: word processing and online research engines such as Google. Both save a great deal of time and energy, increasing paper writing and research efficiency. When I was an undergraduate, we typed and retyped and re-retyped; if while doing our final drafts at 3 a.m. we noticed a missing or incomplete reference, we could not Google it. Rather, we needed to get to the library and find the reference before we handed in the paper at 10 a.m. At the same time, despite the assistance of word processing and Google, greater demands from extra-curricular activities, including community participation, give many students less time to do their academic work.

I am often asked, "What exactly does a humanities professor teach?" Since the answer varies from teacher to teacher, I will respond with what I teach, discuss my goals and philosophy of teaching, and present my observations on the art of teaching.

What Literature Does

It is somewhat old-fashioned to claim that we understand life better by reading imaginative literature. Yet I contend that we do. Non-fiction helps us know more about our world and its past; imagined literature – fiction, poetry, and drama – helps us understand both ourselves and the world beyond ourselves. To say this is not only to agree with Matthew Arnold that literature presents a criticism of life, but also to go much further by arguing that reading literature is a crucial part of life along with experiencing the visual arts, music, architecture, live theater, and film.

Reading is a kind of travel, an imaginative voyage undertaken while sitting still. Reading is immersion; reading is reflection. Reading takes us elsewhere, away from where we live to other places. We read to satisfy our curiosity about other times and places, to garner information about what is happening in the world beyond ourselves, to gather the courage to try new things (even while considering the admonitions not to try dangerous ones), and to learn about experiences and activities that we might try in the future.

Our reading helps us formulate narratives – of personal hopes, plans, putative triumphs, and alternatives to disappointments – that enables us to understand better our pasts and to make plans for our futures. When reading, we extend our horizons; we come to understand what it is like to be of a different gender, race, and class, and to have a different way of looking at things. As Wallace Stevens put it in "The Idea of Order at Key West," words enable us to discover "ourselves and our origins" and perhaps to perceive what Stevens calls "ghostlier demarcations" and "keener sounds" than we may find in our own lives.

We read because we are curious and wish to learn other ways humans organize life, not only in our own culture but also in others. We read to supplement our life experience, and that perhaps includes reconfiguring the values we have been taught. We read for company when we are lonely, for solace when we are in pain. We read to recuse ourselves from the slings and arrows of outrageous fortune and the challenges of our lives; paradoxically, we read to become more alert to those challenges.

But we also read for fun. We read not only to alleviate pain but also for amusement. We read to relax from the pressures of our everyday world. We also read to delight ourselves, to vicariously experience pleasures, joys, sensuality, and passion.

Reading, we must not forget, is also a kind of play. We read to enjoy the pleasure of words, their sensuality and materiality, the smells and tastes and visions they evoke, the desires they elicit, the laughter – as well as the tears and even physical disgust and pain – they arouse.

Anyone who doubts the value of reading needs to read Azar Nafisi's *Reading "Lolita" in Tehran: A Memoir* (2003). Nafisi speaks eloquently of the power of books to transform lives at a time in Tehran when many universities were closed and Western canonical texts were forbidden. She showed her female students what reading can mean by using *The Great Gatsby*, *Lolita*, and other works to open up a world in which personal relationships and their cost are more important than political and religious dogma. What her book teaches us is that literature can have urgency and significance by raising crucial issues that touch on our very existence as humans.

Reading "Lolita" in Tehran reminds us that the stakes of reading major works can be high and that reading can open the doors to other ways of living. We are reminded that it is necessary to read – and not only in a repressive autocracy – in order to see the world from different perspectives and to know the desires and needs of those who are different from ourselves. Finally, each of us reads a literary work differently because each of us comes to a work with different experiences – something reading teaches us both in our responses to a book and in the human differences depicted in books.

I teach how to read closely. My mantra, as noted earlier, is "Always the text; always historicize," by which I mean we should respond to the words on the page as well as consider the author's life and the historical period in which he or she lived as well as the historical period about which he or she wrote. By responding to the words on the page, I mean attending to the power of language as it creates meaning, and being aware of the conscious and unconscious decisions that give a literary work its formal organization, its evolving process, and its effects on readers.

Form refers to the *how* of literature and content refers to the *what*. Form signifies, or, put another way, there is an inextricable relationship between form and content. The significant form of a literary work enacts values that we take from the work.

By form I mean the choices an author consciously – and sometimes unconsciously – makes to shape content: narrative voice, plot structure, patterns of language (image, syntax, and diction), and characterization (how characters are depicted). I eschew a narrow formalism that disdains content – that is, themes and character development – but I also downplay reading that stresses themes separate from form.

History includes the power relationships among classes, genders, and ethnicities – what is sometimes called the New Historicism – but it also includes other cultural productions that contribute to the Zeitgeist. These productions include other art forms – theater, music, the visual arts – and in more recent times, photography, television, and, of course, the Internet. In the case of twentieth-century literature, can we understand multiple perspectives as cultural phenomena without understanding Cubism and its resolution of multiple perspectives on one spatial plane?

There are many ways that literature becomes part of our life experience and thereby contributes not only to the joy of learning but also to the practicality of learning:

1. We identify with the narrative voice or we distance ourselves from that voice, be it a first-person speaker or an omniscient narrator.
2. In much the same way, we identify with or distance ourselves from characters.

3. Reading imaginative literature – as well as such non-fiction as history and biography – enhances our life experience by taking us into other worlds.
4. Reading imaginative literature as well as non-fiction enhances our political and moral awareness.
5. Imagined works complement and often deepen our historical knowledge; paradoxically, this may even take place when the facts are not exactly accurate, if the text speaks to the warp and woof of lived life at a particular time and considers why and how people behave.
6. Imaginative literature is an important part of the history of ideas and enacts important philosophical inquiries and positions.
7. Whether reading imaginative literature or non-fiction, we learn about authors' psyches and values and the way that they saw the world and why.
8. Imaginative literature, along with history, biography, autobiography, and diaries, increases the pleasures of our travels and vice versa.

I believe in masterworks, and believe that the time spent on works like Tolstoy's *War and Peace,* Melville's *Moby Dick*, Joyce's *Ulysses*, and Eliot's *The Waste Land* repays itself. There is a joy in reading and comprehending difficult works. I find a particular joy in teaching and sharing difficult works with students and watching them gradually deepening their comprehension of them. We never "master" masterworks because we bring new experiences to each reading, and such works yield something fresh on each rereading.

The Classroom as an Intellectual Opportunity

I should acknowledge that I am privileged to teach excellent students. During three professorships at the flagship research campus of one state university and important campuses of two others, I have done some teaching of commuting students who have less time to do their academic work. But I want to stress that the model and values I am proposing worked not only at Cornell but also in those visiting situations.

I like to think of the subtitle of my classes as *Cornell Optics*. I believe every undergraduate class should in part be a course in which the professor seeks to sharpen perspicacity so as to help students understand more. I call attention on a regular basis, both on the course listserv and in class, to the vast variety of concerts, lectures, films, and writing opportunities in newspapers and magazines that are part of Cornell University. I have done the same when teaching elsewhere.

At Cornell, I utilize the resources on campus: the art museum, the plays performed at the Cornell Center for Performing Arts, films showing at the campus cinema, and the architecture and design of university buildings. I invite the students to join me at some performances and am fortunate enough to have a campus financial resource that provides complementary theater tickets. In many of my courses, I have at least one class session in the campus Johnson Art Museum. In my freshman class, I use a writing assignment in which I ask the class to compare specific works they have read with specific paintings or sculptures. In other classes, such assignments provide possible topics for sustained essays.

Before my classes at the art museum, I ask each student to select a work that he or she will discuss. Classes at the art museum emphasize the distinction between the spatiality of the visual and the temporality of literary arts, while also showing students that, contrary to what many have thought, painting and sculpture may have a narrative element, while literature may have spatial organization.

While not a substitute for office hours and discussion before and after classes, online communication has introduced new ways of effective teaching. One advantage to listservs and online blackboards is that they give us teachers access to students beyond the classroom. Furthermore we can correspond on email with individual students. When I give a writing assignment in all but freshman classes, I ask every student to send me a paper prospectus, on which I comment and for which I suggest a bibliography. I encourage them to submit outlines and drafts, and respond, after I hand the graded paper back, to my comments – or, depending on the class size, to those of my graduate student reader or teaching assistant.

Teaching Goals

I take my challenge as a teacher to get students to think in sophisticated terms while they write on subjects generated by the reading assignments. Let me say at the outset that I believe in directed discussions focused on the material the students read and the papers they write. I think of myself as an orchestra conductor trying to get the most out of each player and working with each individual to bring out his or her talent. We know that if a student finds a mentor or two in his or her college career, that student will usually have a better experience, and we faculty teaching freshman seminars need to be accessible to fill that role.

My pedagogical goals are:

1. Instill the joy of learning and in particular the joy of reading, in part by sharing my appreciation and understanding of the texts I teach.
2. Teach students to write lucidly and logically and teach them to make an argument that uses examples of close reading to support concepts *and* uses historical and cultural contexts. I seek to teach precision of thought, clarity of expression, logic of argument, and individuality of voice – individuality that may include controlled passion.

153

3. Encourage students to think independently and challenge accepted truths when they think them wrong or in need of modification.
4. Teach students how to compare, contrast, and synthesize. This skill is transferable to other courses and inquiries beyond our particular subject matter.
5. Teach students to read closely and well, to be alert to nuances in language, and to see the *value of reading* in a visual age. Close reading – attention to verbal nuances from tone to phonics – teaches attentiveness to language in writing and in speech.
6. Teach students to articulate ideas orally. I do this by giving them a chance to make presentations in class, even if these are only for a few minutes. As teachers we need to develop student skills that are transferable not only to other disciplines, but also to students' future endeavors, no matter what career and/or educational path they pursue.

In the humanities, given the dearth of college teaching positions, we need to place less emphasis on pre-professional skills that prepare students for a Ph.D. program and more emphasis on reading, writing, and communication skills that will prepare students for a wide variety of career choices. Our goals should include producing adults who not only participate in civic life and help bridge the gap between universities and the educated public, but who also become influential decision-makers in the cultural and political world.

Indeed we need to keep our humanities undergraduate students aware of alternative career paths, including university administrative positions, educational and public policy non-profits, and even journalism, perhaps in the latter case with a focus on the humanities and higher education.

Teaching Writing

While most of my writing instruction takes place in freshman classes – and these are classes composed of Cornell freshmen with advanced placement credentials – I do some writing instruction in upper class courses, both in the classroom and on the course listserv. But much of what follows in this section derives from my teaching seminars in Cornell's freshman writing program, where writing papers is a continuous activity throughout the term.

When students participate as a community in carefully constructing paragraphs on the blackboard, they learn how to discuss difficult and sophisticated texts in lucid sentences. Usually, the workshop focus is on one or two problems derived from the prior set of essays such as the need for more use of the active voice or ways of organizing evidence to make forceful arguments. In this workshop aspect of the freshman writing course, I stress strong conceptual topic sentences, sentence variety, use of evidence, and a taut evolving argument. I focus on these writing goals in all my courses.

I stress in all my classes the importance of synthesizing, contextualizing, and integrating discussion of a specific text with other texts and knowledge, perhaps from other fields. In a typical writing instruction class, we might work together to examine how to use evidence from the text, and how to structure a paragraph that moves sequentially from a concept to a middle level of discourse that negotiates between the concept and specific evidence. Presenting that evidence might include a quotation, followed by a precise comment in terms of the argument, to perhaps more evidence and comment. The paragraph might conclude with a return to a middle level of discourse and finally come back to the original concept.

I should make it clear that when I teach freshman writing, I teach two 75-minute classes a week, and that the classes meet Tuesday and Thursday or Monday and Wednesday. Graded papers are always handed back to students the very next class after they are received. In the first few weeks, when the students are not overwhelmed by other work, I assign shorter papers with shorter intervals between assignments and due dates. When we begin the longer assignments, papers are due nine days later.

In this freshman class – and occasionally in other classes – I do what I call *needs-based assignments* – that is, assignments based on the students' progress. Some students might continue to write shorter essays; some might revise more essays than others; some might propose topics that are a little outside the typical rubric of papers for an assignment. In addition to one stipulated revision assignment, each student may revise as often as he or she wishes. The original grade is not erased, but the second and subsequent grades are recorded. Once a term I give students the option of writing a short story so they can see how to handle point of view, characterization, development, and beginnings and endings. Most take this option.

Teaching Reading

My interests in narratology and in modern art inform my teaching as well as the books I write. I acknowledge the place of resistant reading perspectives – that is, perspectives that *resist* the point of view that authors (or painters) thought they were expressing and building into their work. Often these resistant readings contribute rich feminist, gay, ecological, minority, and other multicultural perspectives that the authors ignored. Certainly our student body has evolved over the years I have been teaching at Cornell into a much richer and more varied group where *difference* is respected. With these changes came changes in how we discuss reading assignments and the writing topics we assign. For example, discussion of the homoerotic implications of male bonding plays a larger role in my discussion of

155

Joseph Conrad's "The Secret Sharer" than it once did. Thus the canon changes, even if the names of the texts are the same.

Without using much of the jargon of contemporary criticism, I differentiate in class between different traditional and more recent critical approaches and define deconstructive, Marxist, new historical, cultural studies, and, especially, feminist approaches. When we discuss texts, I try to make the students aware of what approaches we are using. Thus when we study *To the Lighthouse* by Virginia Woolf, we focus particularly on issues of writing and reading as a woman and on how gender identity affects the text.

Building the Bridge between Reading and Writing in Freshman Classes

Close reading of complex creative texts teaches that style enacts values, that the expectations of audiences change, and that *every choice* a writer makes affects how an audience reads his or her text. I discuss the first stories we read in terms of formal issues related to point of view and narrative voice, and show how they reveal the world in which the speaker lives. Because these texts address problems of unreliable and imperceptive narrators, we discuss degrees of reliability and perceptivity. Later, I move on to third-person omniscient narrators. Part of the reason I stress voice and persona is to make my students aware of how, when they are writing essays or imaginative works of their *own*, structures and choices of language enact their voices and personae.

While acknowledging that scientific writing has different requirements than expository writing – and STEM papers usually use the passive voice – I stress the need for the active voice in most expository writing. If students use the active voice to describe the author's creative decisions and the narrator's self-dramatizing role, they become more aware of how creative and polemical authors make decisions that affect readers' responses, and they learn the difference between authorial and resistant readings. In discussion, to increase the emphasis on the creative act of writing, I insist that students use more accurate terminology to describe what is going on within a text instead of the clichéd and unspecified "it says" or "they say."

While discussing literary works, I not only emphasize the issues I want addressed in the papers, but also demonstrate how a paper on the particular assignment or – if I give a choice among topics, as I do after the first paper or two – assignments might be structured. Sometimes I assign papers asking students to discuss works we have not yet covered, but to do so in terms of issues we have been considering. Other times – particularly when we are addressing complex texts, such as Dostoevsky's *Notes from Underground* – I ask them to build on issues within a text that we have been discussing.

Creating a Community of Inquiry

I wish all my classes to be more than sites where I set assignments and the students then do them only to fulfill a course requirement on the way to getting course credit. I want my classes to be learning communities. Needless to say, this is a goal for which we teachers all strive but often fall short. But I should like to suggest how we might develop a community of inquiry where each student understands learning as a process, takes responsibility for being prepared each day, takes assignments seriously, feels part of a functioning group, and writes his or her essays with a sense of pride in his or her work and evolving writing voice.

Let me return to my freshman class. When we do a short reading assignment, I ask about half the class members to report orally on specific subjects. When I teach novellas or the one longer novel, I might ask the entire class to prepare different subjects. Thus for James Joyce's short but challenging story "Araby," two students might address the retrospective telling, another the beginning, another the end, someone else the theme of Catholicism, another student the theme of empire, two others might be asked to think of the issue of guilt and how it shapes the retrospective teller, another would focus on the role of women, and yet another the speaker's prepubescent psychosexuality. When two students are assigned the same subject, I encourage them to talk to one another and work together. The students might be called upon to make a very short presentation to the class on their assigned subject or they may be called upon during discussion.

I teach writing in the spirit of, "This is true, isn't it?" and try to eschew the dogmatism about writing to which my generation and some of our students have been exposed. For does not the House of Good Writing have many rooms? My goal is to encourage each student to find his or her own voice rather than homogenize all student voices into one Proper Compositional Style. While I do not require it, I suggest keeping a loose-leaf journal, alternating days of writing about personal life with days writing about political and campus issues – or whatever is of interest to the student. I offer to read the journal pages during and/or after the course is over. Interestingly, a number of students have taken up this suggestion after the course – and after the demands of their first or second college semester have lessened – and brought me their journals to read.

My goal is to have every student take part in discussion in at least two classes out of three. Once students begin to participate, they rarely stop. When they participate (rather than sit in the bleachers and watch), they feel better about themselves and the class. The class becomes each student's own experience, not something he or she observes as a bystander. More importantly, when students articulate ideas, they often are using the occasion to clarify those ideas for themselves, and that clarification continues when listening to ensuing responses to their contributions.

The digital world has changed teaching for the better, opening up new ways of bridging the gap between the dorm room and the classroom, and creating an exciting nexus between the two sites. On the first meeting of the freshman course, I collect email addresses and establish a course listserv; each student is expected to make four substantive contributions to an online discussion of course material. To focus the discussion, I propose study questions on each text and on relationships among texts. Many students contribute more often than the four required times.

Indeed, as the term progresses and the students become better readers, the colloquies on email are often stunning, not only in their thoughtfulness and sophistication but also in the precision, lucidity, and energy of their writing. At the end of the term, along with their essays, the students submit their email contributions in their folders. I might add that students are overwhelmingly enthusiastic about the listserv. I encourage both email comments addressed to the entire class and, although they don't count as part of the required four, individual off-list dialogues with me.

Students, and especially freshmen, look to their teachers in small classes as mentors more than they do to their formal advisors. We teachers need to make clear that we are accessible to them in office hours and open to email and phone inquiries. I answer email several times a day from home, and I am also accessible by phone from 8 a.m., to 10 p.m. In addition, the students tend to write each other "off-list," and that is exactly what I want. I have no problem with a student showing a draft to a friend or roommate or other class member, as long as the student writes his or her own paper.

The listserv has another important function in building a community of inquiry. Students are also encouraged to share with the class information about concerts, plays, or sporting events in which they participate; as a result, students attend one another's activities and build commitment to our community.

One way that a class becomes a community of inquiry is regular and prompt attendance, even for classes beginning at 8:40. We *need* to have rules for attendance and make a show of knowing who is present. The last time I taught freshmen, I had over the entire term less than one absence per student, and more than half the students did not miss a class. I usually arrive early and, as the class assembles, I ask what films they have seen and share my views of films I have seen. At other times we might discuss Cornell theater plays or campus issues, or adult choices with which freshmen are faced such as whether to join a fraternity or sorority and how to organize time among the demands of school work, activities, and part-time jobs.

In these pre-class discussions, which, on occasion, overflow into the first few minutes of our 75-minute class period, I might mention what resources are available to students who are having trouble with any of their courses. Or I might discuss how to address difficulties with study habits or time management, particularly at hectic times before midterms and finals. At the end of each month, a few students or I bring a little food for a brief class party, and, while nibbling for 15 minutes, we discuss films, course issues, or topical Cornell and national issues. At the end of term, I give students an informal reading list, suggesting further reading of authors we have read as well as of authors we have not read, especially if they are related to those we have studied.

I offer to read the students' work in the future after the course is over. I remind them that when they read, they should always be aware of the way a piece is written. For examples of good (but not always faultless) writing, I suggest that they should continue to read the editorial page and the Op-Ed page in the *New York Times* and perhaps the *New Yorker,* the *New York Review of Books,* and the *Economist.*

We often have class reunions the next semester, and sometimes these reunions continue for four years. Since the listservs remain in place, class members and I continue to write one another after the class is over. Many of the students whom I teach will take other classes from me, some become my major advisees, and quite often we keep in touch beyond their graduation, sometimes for decades.

A Few Observations about Teaching

(1) Prospective teachers should observe *their* teachers; graduate students should be attentive to their teachers' pedagogy. As a young professor, I learned from watching the professors considered to be the most effective teachers, and indeed I still do.

(2) You need to find your own style and voice.

(3) Teaching is a matter of knowing your audience and interacting with them; your audience will respond to you if you speak passionately about a subject that you care about, know about, and want to continue to learn about. Even knowing is not sufficient if you don't convey the joy of teaching.

(4) Can teaching be taught? We as senior mentors can teach a pretty good teacher to be a much better teacher, and a good teacher to be even better, but I am not sure we can teach someone to be an inspiring teacher for most students. But know that no teacher is great for every student.

(5) Teachers make hundreds of decisions every class period: whom to call on, how to answer a question, and how long to devote to it. We all make mistakes and decisions we regret. When we look back on the day's teaching – something we all need to do – we should probably write in our notes for that class lesson what decisions and strategies could have been better.

(6) Most teachers will get over nervousness and self-consciousness. If not, they are probably not going to be good teachers.

(7) To an extent, our students perform up to our expectations. If you expect students to attend class and be prepared, you need to take attendance and on occasion give a quiz or call on students who don't speak (unless, as does happen, you have a student who will be in emotional pain if you do so). I make clear that on-time attendance and full preparation for each day's class are course requirements.

Conclusion: The Classroom as a Community of Inquiry

My goal is to transform a class into a community of inquiry in which students commit themselves not only to the teacher and to the course material, but also to each other in a spirit of learning. In a community of inquiry, the class does not stop when students and teachers separate and the course ends. The students speak to one another outside the classroom and on email about their reading and writing, and carry their intellectual relationships beyond the life of the course.

What I described as building a community of inquiry is an important aspect in all my classes, but these factors are even more important in classes with a large number of students. I have used what I have been describing in classes with as many as 100 students. Thus in my Modernism lecture course – which in very recent years I limit to 30 but once had enrollments approaching 100 or so – I have a listserv to which all students are required to make three substantive contributions, and these contributions often result in an exciting dialogue about interpretive issues. I make brief comments off-list thanking students for their contribution. I respond rapidly to off-list queries about assignments. I send regular letters to the entire class with study questions and assignments. To get to know each student in the course, I try to come early and chat with a few different students before each class. As in my freshman writing seminar, I offer students a chance to join my wife and me as our guests for Cornell theater, dance, and musical events. In all my classes, I invite my students to dinner three or four times a term at the residential college where I am a House Fellow. To build a community of inquiry, you need to be part of it.

Especially in the humanities, we need to stress learning as an end in itself and as a lifelong odyssey so that our students, as Constantine Cavafy put it,

> Keep Ithaka always in mind.
> Arriving there is what you're destined for.
> ...
> Ithaka gave you the marvelous journey.
> Without her you would not have set out.
> ...
> Wise as you will have become, so full of experience,
> you will have understood by then what these Ithakas mean.
>
> ("Ithaka")

Students need understand that Cornell – and life – is composed of many Ithacas and that these Ithacas represent the wonder of learning.

19

Changing the World One Step at a Time: Comparing Contemporary Students with Those of the Explosive 1968–1970 Period

The current generation of undergraduates are apathetic narcissists who think only about themselves and not about the world and their relationship to it.

Beginnings

At a dinner party some years ago, I heard the above dismissive comment from a retired professor from another university. With regret, he recalled the halcyon days of the late sixties when he and his fellow idealistic students participated in peace marches and thought of revolution that would change not only American foreign policy and the staid university, but also the capitalist system itself. Regretting his own teaching career, he argued that students today learn little in the classroom. Rather cynically, he claimed that what teachers want from students is that the students replicate the teachers' values.

Thinking of Cornell students whom I have taught since coming to Cornell in fall 1968 as well as those I have taught as a visiting professor for a semester or a year, and those I have met when lecturing at other universities or in my travels, I strongly took issue with him.

It is simplistic to contend that in 1968–70 we had an activist student Reformation and that in recent years we have been having a Counter-Reformation defined by ironic detachment from the world beyond the self. The notion, fostered recently by William's Deresiewicz *Excellent Sheep*, that today's college students

How to Succeed in College and Beyond: The Art of Learning, First Edition. Daniel R. Schwarz.
© 2016 John Wiley & Sons, Ltd. Published 2016 by John Wiley & Sons, Ltd.

are interested only in making money and are going through a period of extreme narcissism and apathy about the wider world contradicts what I see every day.

To be sure, students are interested in a fulfilling career, but a great many choose paths that will contribute to society. Those who choose law often go into public interest law and are concerned with protecting the rights of under-served communities, whether they be the minorities or the physically challenged, or the often-voiceless poor. Those who choose medicine often do so to pursue research on possible cures for diseases or to serve communities as family practitioners or emergency room doctors, neither of which are particularly lucrative, especially outside large cities. Many students choosing more financially rewarding fields in business or finance expect to give back in terms of community participation and philanthropy.

Perhaps we can say, "Evolution has replaced Revolution." My students today are very concerned with sustainability and other environmental issues as well as racism, sexism, sexual abuse, unfair labor practices, and terrorism. Perhaps more of their focus is on local issues that they can affect rather than on international issues they cannot affect. Many students begin in high school to volunteer to work with the aged, the physically and emotionally challenged, and the economically disadvantaged and continue public service commitments in college. I have even known students who, while attending college, have served as volunteer firefighters in the Ithaca community.

Looking Backward: The Way We Were in 1968–1970

Refracted through the lens of memory, some remember the turbulence of the 1968–70 period as a time when universities and their students reconstituted themselves, and the world changed because of it. Those who participated in 1968–9 and 1969–70 protests almost half a century ago have a nostalgic perspective on those feisty days, even though most of them have led conventional lives, pursued rather traditional careers, and in many cases are now retired or are close to retirement.

At Cornell, in spring 1969, in response not only to a cross burning at Wari House, a black women's student residence, but also to racial tensions throughout the academic year – including disciplinary actions handed down by the campus judicial system against protesting African-American students – Willard Straight Hall, Cornell's student union building, was seized on April 19 by African-American students.[1]

On April 20, pictures of armed black students exiting Willard Straight sent shivers through the campus and the entire nation, although it was later claimed that the weapons were a defensive measure in response to rumors that armed white students or police would storm the building. In fact, 20 to 25 members of Delta Upsilon fraternity did attempt to take back the building from the armed students. The administration then agreed to the black students' demands and offered them a full amnesty. After an April 21 faculty meeting (which I attended), the faculty passed by voice vote a vague resolution to review African-American student complaints but refused to dismiss the penalties imposed by the judicial system, thus raising the possibility that the amnesty would not be carried out. A meeting of the SDS (Students for a Democratic Society, a left-wing organization) in Barton Hall – one of the main Cornell campus athletic facilities – evolved into a student takeover of that building. In response, the history and government departments refused to teach until order was restored. Much of the faculty and student body lost confidence in James A. Perkins, the President of the university, and he resigned.

Let us turn now to the following year at Cornell. In 1969–70, the campus experienced the crosswinds of two forms of turbulence. Racial tensions were again exacerbated when the African Center was mysteriously burned down on April 1, 1970 and a campus protest, including some looting, ensued. On April 30, President Nixon announced on television a joint US–Saigon offensive into Cambodia with the goal of driving North Vietnamese forces from Cambodia. On May 1, protests erupted on campuses across the US. On May 4, when a national guardsman opened fire on protestors at Kent State and killed four students, 900 colleges and universities, including Cornell, shut down.

David Ruppert, Cornell Professor of Statistics in the Engineering College and Cornell BA '70 with a major in math, recalls that there was a sense that "If we don't change the world, Cornell will not matter." Students challenged professorial authority even as they challenged political authority; they wanted to remake the university to fit their needs and sought a strong voice in that remaking. Many departments held teach-ins where students expressed their dissatisfaction with what they felt was an oppressive educational system emphasizing grades and exams.

My retrospective understanding of those years is complex. Education has always been a balance between inside and outside the classroom. Some healthy dents were made in the notion of the professor as the unquestioned emperor of knowledge. But reconstituting classrooms as teach-ins and communes where authority supposedly ceased to exist and every view, no matter how violent or foolish, was given equal weight – something tried in the later stages of the spring terms in 1969 and 1970 – didn't serve much of an educational purpose. If you believed in what you were doing – in my case, teaching students how to read great literature perceptively and insightfully, how to write lucidly and precisely, and how to think critically – it was not a plus to disrupt the university's learning process during the final weeks of two consecutive academic years.

It is worth remembering that many and perhaps most students were not active participants in student protests, and whatever their memories, most did not go on the various marches to Washington. I do recall that many more students did participate in various anti-war protests than in anti-university protests. Many if not most students and faculty believed that political protest could co-exist with traditional learning, but they were somewhat cowed by others who insisted on disrupting the educational process. Dismayed by the Vietnam War, I had attended peace vigils while doing my Ph.D. studies at Brown. In the overheated crucible of the 1968 and 1969 protests, I witnessed, along with splendid idealism, some intolerance, bullying, and sanctimoniousness.

Paradoxically, within the tent of non-conformity in the 1968–70 period, there was in fact much conformity and some demagoguery. I recall how at various political meetings, one had to shout "Power to the People" with a raised arm and a closed fist or be shouted down. Many faculty were frightened when in the spring of 1969, Harry Edwards, then a graduate student at Cornell, came dressed in military fatigues to a meeting of a group called Concerned Faculty who were sympathetic to rescinding the punishment meted out to black students. At that meeting, Edwards spoke of having his "piece" (meaning his gun) in the pocket of his fatigues. And I remember how in spring 1970, faculty were asked to stand fire-watch because of the threat that the campus would be physically destroyed.

With a handful of exceptions, most of the politically active 1968–70 Cornell students I knew have made traditional lives, which in many cases include a good deal of commendable community conscientiousness. Notable is Tom Jones, who became a major figure in TIAA-CREF (a financial services company which specializes in serving the education community) and a Cornell Trustee; many others became professors, doctors, lawyers, and community leaders. Some students returned to Cornell after dropping out, including Simeon Moss, who returned to college and became Press Relations Office Director at Cornell.

To be sure, a few of the students I knew became permanent members of the counterculture as blacksmiths, massage therapists, and founding members of the Moosewood Collective, which still runs the Moosewood restaurant in Ithaca. In addition to those who lived successfully for some years with one foot in the counterculture and the other in the mainstream culture or returned to the mainstream after some years on the fringe, there were a small group who did get lost in that period's time warp and never got it together in terms of a traditional life or career.

What Did Those Explosive Years Contribute to Today's Student Life? How Is University Life Different Now as a Result?

The immediate effect of those tumultuous times upon ensuing years was that the university created programs and policies to pursue issues that were raised in 1968–70. Gradually, in the decades that followed, the range of courses has expanded. Courses in popular culture – the 1960s, History of Rock, Hip-Hop, Jazz, Baseball in American culture – draw well, especially with a first-rate lecturer. Courses range in the English Department from African-American Literature, Asian-American Literature, and African Literature to courses in Queer Theory and one entitled "Transgender and Transexuality." Courses entitled "Desire" and "Decadence" have a strong following, in part because of a charismatic professor.

The curriculum has evolved in response to the issues raised in the 1960s to take account not only of identity politics – women's, black, and gay studies – but also of new and rapidly evolving fields, especially in STEM fields where students might get employment. Perhaps learning for its own sake as opposed to learning that furthers a career goal is less a feature of the Cornell experience than it once was. But those students I know still take liberal arts courses for the pleasure of learning.

The curriculum is a bit less imposed by faculty and develops more in response to students' professional needs, curiosity, and interests; in other words it is some-what more customer-oriented. Curricular changes reflect a greater focus on what employers are looking for, not only because that is what students want, but also because the efficacy and reputation of universities are measured by the accomplishments of their students. For example, at elite engineering colleges, research and curriculum are now focused more on entrepreneurship and sustainability; this focus is part of a greater emphasis in engineering on areas of practical application rather than on theoretical concerns. Thus the fledgling Cornell Tech in NYC advertises: "We bring academics and the tech community together to develop transformative ideas and talent, and encourage creative vision, technical depth and entrepreneurial thinking. We envisioned how edu-cation could meet tech needs now and in the future, then developed a powerful curriculum to put that into practice." Cornell Associate Professor of Electrical and Computer Engineering David Delchamps observes: "While I agree that focus on entrepreneurship and sustainability has increased, I see the change more as a shift in emphasis for the practical/application side of engineering rather than a turn away from theory per se."

Challenges to professorial authority, while often more subtle, have become a part of the learning process. If students are more accepting today than in 1969–70, they are not as quiescent as most were in the early and mid-sixties when I was a graduate student at Brown from 1963 to 1968, and even earlier when I was an undergraduate at Union College from 1959 to 1963. But even in the early sixties, activist students played an important role in the civil rights movement.

Some of the interrogative spirit in the 1970s and the ensuing years derives from the questioning of authority in 1968–70, a questioning that has been modified and transfigured but has not disappeared and makes the classroom and campus life livelier and more exciting. Today's students are vocally concerned with the environment, sexual harassment, economic inequality, and educational opportunity. As a result of courses with a feminist inflection and feminist political activity, women students are more confident and speak more frequently in class. In my early teaching days, I often had women students who were a good deal brighter and better prepared than they thought they were, but they were intimidated by male students who were less bright and not as well prepared as they thought they were.

How Has the Undergraduate Student Body Changed?

Partly as a response to both local and national events of the late 1960s, we have much greater ethnic variety on campus. Today's students are more respectful of diversity and difference. Gay students are far more open, in part because at most colleges the community is far more accepting of gay students and gay faculty as well as of transgender and transsexual students. While there is always room for improvement, students are more comfortable about who they are in terms not only of sexual preference, but also of their ethnicity and their relationship to those of different ethnicities and socio-economic backgrounds. This leads to more interracial social interaction – including dating and relationships – than in the past. These trends toward tolerance begin in high school and even in primary school as well as within students' own homes.

Another aspect of diversity that is found at many universities and colleges is the presence of more foreign students – and from more countries, including non-European ones – among the undergraduates than there were even 15 years ago; this change breeds awareness that there are different cultural and political values than those in the US.

Diversity takes many forms, including facilities for the physically challenged. Buildings are wheelchair accessible; special parking spaces exist for the handicapped and those who need to park closer to the buildings in which they work. We have professionals on the Cornell staff who come to class and take notes for the deaf; provisions are made for seeing-eye dogs to accompany the blind into buildings where dogs are not otherwise allowed. Jewish students have access to kosher dining, and there are significant choices of meals – vegetarian, gluten free, etc. – to satisfy different needs and preferences. Indeed, in its "Options for Dining on Campus," Cornell proclaims: "Students following vegetarian, vegan, kosher, Halal, Muslim, Seventh-day Adventist, and other diets will find delicious dining options all over campus."

The rise in tuition has affected the demography of the Cornell student body less than one might expect. Total financial aid has increased dramatically. With soaring tuition costs, more students qualify for financial aid. Cornell gives scholarship support to more than 45 percent of its students, often in combination with loan packages; the latter are far smaller in dollars because Cornell does not want its graduates overburdened by debt. Other students have various forms of outside aid. Often, first-generation scholarship students fertilize the university meritocracy and demography. A handful of years ago I taught a wonderful student who was the first member of her family to go to college; her father's union, Theatrical Teamsters 817, gave her a full scholarship.

Students today are more concerned with economics, in part because they live in a more acquisitive society than that of the late 1960s. Many students at that time came from families whose parents grew up in the Depression before entering the middle class. Rather than seek ostentatious wealth, most students seemed happy to achieve middle-class comforts.

Now that the US has emerged – at least in part – from the 2008 economic downturn, I would guess that in 2015 the average undergraduate student comes from a wealthier background than in the late 1960s. Especially in Cornell's endowed colleges (Engineering; Arts and Science; Hotel; Architecture, Art, and Planning) where tuition is higher for New York State residents than in the statutory or land grant colleges (Agriculture and Life Sciences, Industrial and Labor Relations, Human Ecology), many of our contemporary students at Cornell seem to come from prosperous families relatively untouched by economic vicissitudes. For their families, the rising tuition is not a problem.

Many students in the College of Arts and Science – not infrequently alumni children – live lives of great privilege in terms of resources and experience. For example, a much higher percentage of today's students have cars, have been to Europe (often many times), come from families with multiple homes, and live in expensive high-rise apartments in Collegetown – an area of Ithaca adjacent to Cornell – that were built in the last several years. Most of our undergraduate foreign students don't receive aid, and a good many come from privileged backgrounds.

The Way We Are in 2015

Let us consider how the texture of student life is different from that of past generations of students.

The Internet revolution has changed the way we teach and learn. Pauline Shongov, Cornell '18, an especially conscientious and curious student, mentions how in this digital age younger people are so deluged by information that "the trouble now is discerning how to be our personal librarians, that is, choosing and filtering among all the information."

Much research, reading, and learning is now done with the help of the Internet; books and printed newspapers play a smaller role in education. Students depend on the Internet for information, and this cuts down for better or worse the time that they spend on research. So, too, does the time spent writing on a computer versus the old process of typing, retyping and re-retyping papers.

Teaching, too, has changed. The wall between the student's living space and the classroom has dissolved because faculty can communicate asynchronically with students and advisees via listservs and email. As I have mentioned, I ask my students to contribute to a course listserv and I write them a weekly letter that focuses on where we are and where we are going in terms of the syllabus and that provides study questions for reading assignments. During the term, some of my weekly letters focus on paper writing and include bibliographies for further reading.

Students used to take pride in cutting the umbilical cord when they arrived at Cornell. In some ways, students are more independent of their parents, and in some ways less, although, of course, independence varies from student to student. Frequently, "helicopter parents" hover over students, wanting to direct their children's choices and activities.

Several students and parents with whom I have spoken feel that parents "are now less restrictive," and that conforms to my impression. Many students think of parents as friends as much as authority figures. They communicate with their parents much more than in the past and may get far more input than they need. Although some parents believe they are being told everything in a constant stream of emails and cell phone calls, most students selectively confide in them.

For most of today's students, alcohol is the drug of choice, but there is a considerable use of marijuana. According to a recent study in the *Michigan News*:

> Illicit drug use has been rising gradually among American college students since 2006, when 34 percent indicated that they used some illicit drug in the prior year; that rate was up to 39 percent by 2013. Most of this increase is attributable to a rising proportion using marijuana, according to the University of Michigan scientists who conduct the nationwide Monitoring the Future study.

At Cornell and other colleges there are pockets of cocaine use and abuse of prescription drugs.

While the students of 1968–70 lived through the supposed sexual revolution, sex on campus is more open and widespread today. Certainly, if the *Cornell Daily Sun* and various statistics describing the sexual mores of young adults can be believed, students are more sexually free-spirited and experimental than 50 years ago. In recent years, Cornell had a widely attended "sex education" forum on anal sex – "Anal Sex 101: Everything You Wanted to Know (But Were Afraid to Ask)"– with Tristan Taormino; the seminar was sponsored by a variety of campus groups and programs. Taormino gives these seminars on other campuses as well. Every other Thursday, the *Cornell Daily Sun* carries two sexually explicit autobiographical advice columns that would have shocked most students in the late 1960s.

Are Today's Students More Practical and Career-Oriented?

A good deal of my experience with 2008–15 students comes from English majors and other humanities majors. Traditionally, humanities students are not the most materialistic or career-oriented students, although they can be as self-absorbed as other young adults. What I see today are students who wish to contribute to their various communities, but who have a practical awareness of what can be accomplished. They are certainly much more conscious of the environment than earlier generations of students and are more likely to volunteer for programs aimed at educating prisoners or working with local disadvantaged school children. While they are less likely to be involved in political protests, quite a few do work in political campaigns.

Professor Ruppert believes that his recent engineering students are "ambitious, dedicated, hard-working, and excited about their work" but not as "intellectually curious" or "idealistic" as the Cornell students of his own time. To be sure, students are more pragmatic than in the 1968–70 period; many more English majors take economics courses, sometimes at the behest of parents who are worried that their child's English major is a passport to poverty.

Economic downturns and even the fear thereof may be a factor in orienting students to those fields that are more practical. An indication of the practical bent of our English majors is that many are double majors – a handful with an economics major – and quite a few are pre-med or pre-law. But we still have many students who wish to teach at some level and/or become creative writers. Others, most of whom write for the aforementioned *Cornell Daily Sun*, wish to go into journalism; still others are interested in publishing. Students are understandably reluctant to choose academic careers in fields where the job market is tight.

The current generation of students is more focused than earlier generations on what happens next. They are more grade-oriented than in the past, and more often take courses in which the average grades are high; average course grades are often accessible on the Internet. Decisions about courses and summer jobs – including non-paying internships – are often made with career preparation in mind.

But are today's students cynical careerists? Not in my experience. I find today's students more directed and mature and, although more realistic about what they can contribute to saving the world, no less idealistic. They use their time better and accomplish more than any group of students that I have ever taught.

Among the 2008 Magna Cum Laudes in English was Kayla Rakowski Dryden, Cornell '08, who was an Education Intern at Cornell's Johnson Art Museum and President of her sorority, even while doing a splendid honors thesis on "Wallace Stevens and Modern Art." Kayla's parents are both Cornellians from the 1970s. She felt that her father's generation – the generation whose parents were emerging from the Depression – were more focused on their careers, whereas her generation does not feel the same pressure and think more of post-college life as an odyssey wherein one visits a variety of experiences.

Kayla, who now has a position at MoMA after doing an MA in Museum Studies at NYU, saw "Cornell as an opportunity" to develop her potential: "I also feel like my classroom experience was really just one component among many positive components that made up my time on campus.... [T]hrough my leadership roles in clubs and internships.... I came to understand my strengths and weaknesses ... in a more real-world environment."

Perhaps first-generation college students and those from less well-off families are generally more focused on acquiring career skills. Indeed, they are more likely to pursue STEM fields and economics – perhaps in business-focused programs – rather than the humanities. These choices may result in part because first-generation college students sometimes come from families where English is not the first language. This is true now of some Asian families and for some families from the old USSR as it was in a prior era for recently arrived Jewish families who spoke Yiddish.

When I first came to Cornell, the students editing the *Cornell Daily Sun* or acting in plays were often different students from those excelling academically; now they are more likely to be the same. If there is one thing that categorizes today's students, it is not the concern that time is money but, rather, that time is time, and that time is a resource that needs to be used as fruitfully as possible, whether for work, extra-curricular activities, volunteerism, or social life. Most of the students I know are voracious learners, and that voracity extends far beyond classes. I offer my students tickets to plays at the Cornell Center for Performing Arts, and I often have more takers than I have tickets.

Today's students are competent, goal-oriented, and savvy. They communicate by means of cell phone, email, Facebook, Twitter, Instagram, and other social media sites. Yes, students may waste time on these sites and some seem too obsessive about checking them. Yet these sites can be resources for thoughtful exchanges on important issues.

Activism tends to be less visible because Internet access is basically private and students passionately debate issues and organize themselves online. According to Kayla Rakowski Dryden, students use these sources to learn about the possibility of joining active political groups such as in 2008 "A Million Strong for Barack Obama":

We are mavens [experts] in communication – we text, call, blog, instant message, Gchat, comment, and email. ... [I]ssues like global warming, sustainability, the electoral process, education and public health have struck a chord with young people today. We are ... accused of being apathetic, but I really believe that we both care and act.

Anna Dubenko, Cornell '08, observes: "It's axiomatic to say that the Internet has changed the way we communicate and relate to each other. Sometimes ... it draws people together and serves as a catalyst for action and participation."

Are today's students lacking in idealism? I write recommendations every year for some of my best students for Teach For America. In 2007–8 almost 25,000 candidates applied for about 3,700 places. In 2012, 48,000 candidates applied for 5,800 places, and 57,000 candidates applied in 2013 of which 11,000 were chosen with the goal of reaching 750,000 students. Indeed, by 2013, there were already 32,000 alumni teachers from the program. Other recent graduates go into the Peace Corps or go abroad to teach English or become Teaching Fellows in New York.

While these students are compensated, that does not diminish their enormous commitment to the public good. I should add that some critics claim that too many of these students do not pursue a teaching career. Nor do they believe that Teach For America participants add as much as the organization claims to a school's efficacy.

Yes, some students regard these public service activities as intermissions while they decide what career to purse. But, to my mind, that some students use these few years to think about the future does not substantively lessen their idealism.

Conclusion

Students are, like all of us, culturally and historically defined by their era, and their behavior is shaped by a complex grammar of motives. In the past decade, we have had unpopular wars in Iraq and Afghanistan, while in the late 1960s and early 1970s we had the Vietnam War. While these more recent wars may seem far away, they are still very much part of students' consciousness. Many contemporary Cornell students know fellow high school students who are serving or have served in the aforementioned war zones. Our ROTC students have taken up leadership positions in these zones. Now we are facing the horrific behavior and terrorism of ISIS and the possibility of renewed military engagement. If we had a draft, as we did in the 1960s, perhaps the current generation of students would take to the streets to protect their own interests, but what does that say about the inherent pragmatism underlying some of the idealism of the 1960s?

What I am suggesting is that we need to be careful about proposing reductive categories. While each generation of college students is different, they have all been united over my 47 years of teaching by an eagerness to learn and to see college as a way to open doors and windows of understanding themselves and the world in which they live.

On balance, while students today may be more likely to focus on their own personal futures, they also have a strong ethical interest in what they can do as individuals to make the world better. I see many parallels among generations in their idealistic concerns for people in the US and the world. Many students then and now are concerned that all people have their basic needs of food, shelter, and safety fulfilled as well as that all people have the opportunity to live in communities where justice, fairness, self-determination, and political stability are possible.

I close with excerpts from the eloquent response of Ashley Featherstone, Magna Cum Laude in English, Cornell '08, to my invitation to summarize her Cornell experience:

> For me, Cornell was an amazing experience. ... I know that the people I spent the most time with were people who shared many of the same values as me – hard work, determination, integrity, and service. None of the people with whom I associated ever took their success or their opportunities for granted
>
> Whether through music, art, literature, business, science, medicine, etc., [Cornell] students are ready to take on challenges and eager to solve the problems they see in their world. I think they are idealistic, struggling with issues of war, poverty, race, gender, sexuality, education, and the environment.

My sense is that she speaks not only for most Cornellians but also for a great many college students who look at the world as both a challenge and an opportunity.

Note

1   I checked my memory with the "Report of the Special Trustee Committee on Campus Unrest at Cornell."

Works Cited and Select Bibliography

Note: *Many of my sources were emails to me*

Abel, Jaison R. and Richard Deitz. "The Value of a College Degree," *Liberty Street Economics*, September 2, 2014. Accessed August 13, 2015. (http://libertystreeteconomics.newyorkfed.org/2014/09/the-value-of-a-college-degree.html#.VcykpaOFO6o)

American Academy of Arts and Sciences. "The Heart of the Matter," 2013. Accessed August 20, 2015. (http://www.humanitiescommission.org/_pdf/hss_report.pdf)

Apgar, Travis. "Message from Associate Dean of Students Travis Apgar," *Cornell*, 2015. Accessed August 20, 2015. (http://author.dos.cornell.edu/greek/)

Arum, Richard, "A Lack of Rigor Leaves Students 'Adrift' in College." NPR, February 9, 2011. Accessed August 6, 2015. (http://www.npr.org/2011/02/09/133310978/in-college-a-lack-of-rigor-leaves-students-adrift)

Autor, David H. "Skills, Education, and the Rise of Earnings Inequality among the 'Other 99 Percent,'" *Science Magazine Digital*, May 23, 2014. Accessed August 3, 2015. (http://www.sciencemagazinedigital.org/sciencemagazine/23_may_2014?pg=71%20-%20pg71#pg71)

Bellafonte, Gina. "Community College Student Face a Very Long Road to Graduation," *New York Times*, October 3, 2014. Accessed August 4, 2015. (http://www.nytimes.com/2014/10/05/nyregion/community-college-students-face-a-very-long-road-to-graduation.html)

Bergman, Barry. "Higher Ed in Crisis? Make that Plural, Says Veteran Observer," *Berkeley News*, January 30, 2015. Accessed August 3, 2015. (http://newscenter.berkeley.edu/2015/01/30/blumenstyk-cshe/)

Birmingham, Kevin. *The Most Dangerous Book: The Battle for James Joyce's* Ulysses. New York: Penguin, 2014.

How to Succeed in College and Beyond: The Art of Learning, First Edition. Daniel R. Schwarz.
© 2016 John Wiley & Sons, Ltd. Published 2016 by John Wiley & Sons, Ltd.

Works Cited and Select Bibliography

Bloomberg Review. "Dean Wormer's Favorite Editorial," January 7, 2014. Accessed August 6, 2015. (http://www.bloombergview.com/articles/2014-01-07/dean-wormer-s-favorite-editorial)

Blumenstyk, Goldie. *American Higher Education in Crisis? What Everyone Needs to Know.* New York: Oxford University Press, 2014.

Brooks, David. "History for Dollars," *New York Times,* June 7, 2010. Accessed August 11, 2015. (http://www.nytimes.com/2010/06/08/opinion/08brooks.html)

Bruni, Frank. "Demanding More from College," *New York Times,* September 6, 2014. Accessed August 5, 2015. (http://www.nytimes.com/2014/09/07/opinion/sunday/frank-bruni-demanding-more-from-college.html)

Bruni, Frank. *Where You Go Is Not Who You'll Be: An Antidote to the College Admissions Mania.* New York: Grand Central, 2015.

Bryn Mawr. "Bryn Mawr Postbaccalaureate Premedical Program." Accessed August 6, 2015. (http://www.brynmawr.edu/postbac/home.shtml)

Busnaina, Ibrahim. "Avoid 4 Medical School Admission Myths," *US News,* April 11, 2011. Accessed August 3, 2015. (http://www.usnews.com/education/blogs/medical-school-admissions-doctor/2011/04/11/avoid-4-medical-school-admissions-myths)

Campus ESP. Accessed August 11, 2015. (http://www.campusesp.com/)

Carey, Kevin. "Flip Side of Reducing Student Debt Is Increasing the Federal Deficit," *New York Times,* February 10, 2015. Accessed August 4, 2015. (http://www.nytimes.com/2015/02/11/upshot/calculating-the-price-to-taxpayers-of-easing-the-student-debt-burden.html)

Carey, Kevin. *The End of College: Creating the Future of Learning and the University of Everywhere.* New York: Riverhead Books, 2015.

Carey, Kevin. "For Accomplished Students, Reaching a Good College Isn't as Hard as It Seems," *New York Times,* November 29, 2014. Accessed August 4, 2015. (http://www.nytimes.com/2014/11/30/upshot/for-accomplished-students-reaching-a-top-college-isnt-actually-that-hard.html)

Carey, Kevin. "The In-State Tuition Break, Slowly Disappearing," *New York Times,* May 18, 2015. Accessed August 4, 2015. (http://www.nytimes.com/2015/05/19/upshot/the-in-state-tuition-break-slowly-disappearing.html)

Carrns, Ann. "How to Appeal College Financial Aid Officers," *New York Times,* April 24, 2015. Accessed August 4, 2015. (http://www.nytimes.com/2015/04/25/your-money/how-to-appeal-college-financial-aid-offers.html)

Cavafy, Constantine. "Ithaka," Cavafy Archive. Accessed August 11, 2015. (http://www.cavafy.com/poems/content.asp?cat=1&id=74)

CNN. *Ivory Tower* website. Accessed August 4, 2015. (http://edition.cnn.com/shows/ivory-tower)

Codeacademy.com. Accessed August 20, 2015. (https://www.codecademy.com/)

College Confidential. Accessed August 4, 2015. (http://www.collegeconfidential.com/college_search/)

College Parent Central. Accessed August 11, 2015. (http://www.collegeparentcentral.com)

College Parent Central. "Is Your College Student Investing Enough Time Studying?" Accessed August 20, 2015. (http://www.collegeparentcentral.com/2010/02/is-your-college-student-investing-enough-time-studying/)

Common Application. Accessed August 18, 2015. (https://www.commonapp.org/)

Works Cited and Select Bibliography

Complete University Guide. "Applying to a British University." Accessed August 4, 2015. (http://www.thecompleteuniversityguide.co.uk/international/studying-in-the-uk/applying-to-a-british-university/)

Cornell University. "Options for Dining on Campus," Living@Cornell. Accessed August 12, 2015. (https://living.sas.cornell.edu/get_started/housingdiningatcu/optionsfordining/)

The Dartmouth. "Verbum Ultimum: Abolish the Greek System." October 17, 2014. Accessed August 6, 2015. (https://lockerdome.com/6529549357827137/7071761330093332)

Daum, Kevin. "8 Things Really Efficient People Do," *Inc.*, November 1, 2013. Accessed August 4, 2015. (http://www.inc.com/kevin-daum/8-things-really-efficient-people-do.html)

Deresiewicz, William. *Excellent Sheep: The Miseducation of the American Elite and the Way to a Meaningful Life*. New York: Free Press, 2014.

Dirks, Nicholas B. "What 'Ivory Tower' Gets Wrong," *Chronicle of Higher Education*, July 22, 2014. Accessed August 3, 2015. (http://chronicle.com/blogs/conversation/2014/07/22/what-ivory-tower-gets-wrong/)

Doherty, Risa C. "Greek Letters at a Price," *New York Times*, October 28, 2014. Accessed August 6, 2015. (http://www.nytimes.com/2014/11/02/education/edlife/greek-letters-at-a-price.html)

Dostoevsky, Fyodor. *Notes from Underground*, ed. with an introduction by Robert G. Durgy, trans. Serge Shiskoff. New York: Thomas Y. Crowell, 1969.

Dostoevsky, Fyodor. *Crime and Punishment*, trans. Richard Pevear and Larissa Volokhonsky. New York: Vintage, 1993.

Duke, Marshall P. "Starting College: A Guide for Parents: 2013," *Huffington Post*, July 29, 2013. Accessed August 11, 2015. (http://www.huffingtonpost.com/marshall-p-duke/starting-college-a-guide-_b_3670553.html)

"Education." Cornell Tech, Cornell University, 2015. Accessed October 8, 2015. (http://tech.cornell.edu/education).

Ehrenberg, Ronald G. *Tuition Rising: Why College Costs So Much*. Cambridge, Mass.: Harvard University Press, 2000.

FAFSA. Accessed August 4, 2015. (https://fafsa.ed.gov)

Favobooks. "Vladimir Putin's 5 Favorite Books." Accessed August 12, 2015. (http://favobooks.com/politicians/86-vladimir-putin-reads.html)

Federal Stafford Loans. Accessed August 4, 2015. (http://www.staffordloan.com)

Federal Student Aid. Accessed August 4, 2015. (https://studentaid.ed.gov/repay-loans/understand/plans/income-driven)

FinAid. "What Can You Do If Your Parents Can't Help Pay for School?" Accessed August 4, 2015. (http://www.finaid.org/otheraid/parentsrefuse.phtml)

Flanagan, Caitlin. "The Dark Power of Fraternities," *The Atlantic*, March 2014. Accessed August 6, 2015. (http://www.theatlantic.com/magazine/archive/2014/03/the-dark-power-of-fraternities/357580/)

Friedman, Thomas L. "It Takes a Mentor," *New York Times*, September 9, 2011. Accessed August 5, 2015. (http://www.nytimes.com/2014/09/10/opinion/thomas-friedman-it-takes-a-mentor.html)

Ghansah, Rachel Kaadzi. "The Radical Vision of Toni Morrison," *New York Times*, 12 April 2015. Accessed August 12, 2015. (http://www.nytimes.com/2015/04/12/magazine/the-radical-vision-of-toni-morrison.html)

Glassner, Barry and Schapiro, Morton. "Beware Higher-Ed Doomsayers," *Northwestern*, October 8, 2014 (originally published October 6, 2014 in *Chronicle of Higher Education*). Accessed August 3, 2015. (http://www.northwestern.edu/newscenter/stories/2014/10/opinion-chronicle-glassner-schapiro-higher-ed-doomsayers.html)

Glenn, Cheryl and Gray, Loretta, eds. *The Hodges Harbrace Handbook*. 18th edition. Boston: Wadsworth, 2013.

Go Army. Accessed August 4, 2015. (http://www.goarmy.com/reserve/benefits/education.html)

Goldman, Andrew. "Khaled Hosseini on How the Iraq War Hurt Afghanistan," *New York Times*, May 17, 2013. Accessed August 11, 2015. (http://www.nytimes.com/2013/05/19/magazine/khaled-hosseini-on-how-the-iraq-war-hurt-afghanistan.html)

Gopnik, Adam. "Why Teach English?" *New Yorker*, August 27, 2013. Accessed August 11, 2015. (http://www.newyorker.com/books/page-turner/why-teach-english)

Graff, Gerald. *Professing Literature: An Institutional History*. Chicago: University of Chicago Press, 1987.

Grant, Adam. "A Solution for Bad Teaching," *New York Times*, February 5, 2014. Accessed August 12, 2015. (http://www.nytimes.com/2014/02/06/opinion/a-solution-for-bad-teaching.html)

Harpham, Geoffrey Galt. *The Humanities and the Dream of America*. Chicago: University of Chicago Press, 2011.

Haskins, Charles. *The Rise of Universities*. Ithaca, NY: Cornell University Press, 1957.

Herszenhorn, David. "Xenophobic Chill Descends on Moscow," *New York Times*, April 12, 2014. Accessed August 12, 2015. (http://www.nytimes.com/2014/04/13/world/europe/xenophobic-chill-descends-on-moscow.html)

Herzog, Karen. "Survey: College Students Study an Average 15 hours Per Week," *JS Online*, November 15, 2011. Accessed August 6, 2015. (http://www.jsonline.com/blogs/news/133920308.html)

Hoffmann, Roald. "Teach to Search." *Journal of Chemical Education*, 73 (9) 1996: A202–9. Accessed August 12, 2015. (http://pubs.acs.org/doi/pdf/10.1021/ed073pA202)

Jay, Paul and Graff, Gerald. "Fear of Being Useful," *Inside Higher Education*, January 5, 2012. Accessed August 11, 2015. (https://www.insidehighered.com/views/2012/01/05/essay-new-approach-defend-value-humanities)

Kakutani, Michiko. "Wonder Bread and Curry: Mingling Cultures, Conflicted Hearts," *New York Times*, April 4, 2008. Accessed August 11, 2015. (http://www.nytimes.com/2008/04/04/books/04Book.html)

Kaminer, Ariel. "Applications by the Dozen, as Anxious Seniors Hedge College Bets," *New York Times*, November 15, 2014. Accessed August 4, 2015. (http://www.nytimes.com/2014/11/16/nyregion/applications-by-the-dozen-as-anxious-students-hedge-college-bets.html)

Kingkade, Tyler. "Hundreds Call on Dartmouth to Overhaul Its Powerful Greek System," *Huffington Post*, August 13, 2014. Accessed August 6, 2015 (http://www.huffingtonpost.com/2014/08/13/dartmouth-greek-system_n_5673263.html)

Kristof, Nicholas. "Professors, We Need You!" *New York Times*, February 15, 2014. Accessed August 12, 2015. (http://www.nytimes.com/2014/02/16/opinion/sunday/kristof-professors-we-need-you.html)

Kristof, Nicholas. "Starving for Wisdom," *New York Times*, April 16, 2015. Accessed August 11, 2015. (http://www.nytimes.com/2015/04/16/opinion/nicholas-kristof-starving-for-wisdom.html)

Lambert, Lance. "Is a Degree Still Worth It? Yes, Researchers Say, and the Payoff Is Getting Better," *Chronicle of Higher Education*, September 5, 2014. Accessed August 3, 2015. (http://chronicle.com/blogs/data/2014/09/05/is-a-degree-still-worth-it-yes-researchers-say-and-the-payoff-is-getting-better/)

Lemann, Nicholas. "Unhappy Days for America," *New York Review of Books*, 52 (9) May 21, 2015: 25–7. Accessed August 20, 2015. (http://www.nybooks.com/articles/archives/2015/may/21/our-kids-unhappy-days-america/)

Leonhardt, David. "A New Push to Get Low-Income Students Through College," *New York Times*, October 28, 2014. Accessed August 4, 2015. (http://www.nytimes.com/2015/04/26/upshot/college-for-the-masses.html)

Leonhardt, David. "College for the Masses," *New York Times*, April 24, 2015. Accessed August 3, 2015. (http://www.nytimes.com/2015/04/26/upshot/college-for-the-masses.html?hp&action=click&pgtype=Homepage&module=c-column-top-span-region&region=c-column-top-span-region&WT.nav=c-column-top-span-region&abt=0002&abg=1&_r=1)

Lieber, Ron. "A Beginner's Guide to Repaying Student Loans," *New York Times*, May 16, 2014. Accessed August 4, 2015. (http://www.nytimes.com/2014/05/17/your-money/paying-for-college/a-beginners-guide-to-repaying-student-loans.html)

Lieber, Ron. "Navigating the Thickets of Student Loan Counseling," *New York Times*, April 24, 2015. Accessed August 4, 2015. (http://www.nytimes.com/2015/04/25/your-money/the-problem-of-navigating-impenetrable-thickets-of-financial-aid-counseling.html)

Light, Richard J. *Making the Most of College: Students Speak Their Minds*. Cambridge, Mass.: Harvard University Press, 2001.

Mather, Cotton. "Directions for a Son Going to the Colledge," *Congregational Library & Archives*, circa 1718–1719. Accessed August 5, 2015. (http://www.congregationallibrary.org/sites/all/nehh/series2/mathercotton/matherc_lr1.html)

Mayfield, Julie and Lindsey. "7 Considerations When Thinking about Greek Life," *US News*, September 20, 2011. Accessed August 6, 2015. (http://www.usnews.com/education/blogs/twice-the-college-advice/2011/09/20/7-considerations-when-thinking-about-greek-life)

Michaels, Walter Benn. *The Trouble with Diversity: How We Learned to Love Identity and Ignore Inequality*. New York: Holt, 2007.

Michigan News. "College Students' Use of Marijuana on the Rise, Some Drugs Declining," September 8, 2014. Accessed August 12, 2015. (http://ns.umich.edu/new/releases/22362-college-students-use-of-marijuana-on-the-rise-some-drugs-declining)

Mitchell, Josh. "A College Degree Pays Off Far Faster Than It Used To," *Wall Street Journal*, September 2, 2014. Accessed August 3, 2015. (http://blogs.wsj.com/economics/2014/09/02/a-college-degree-pays-off-far-faster-than-it-used-to/)

Nafisi, Azar. *Reading "Lolita" in Tehran: A Memoir.* New York: Random House, 2003.

Olson, Elizabeth. "Burdened with Debt, Law School Graduates Struggle in Job Market," *New York Times*, April 26, 2015. Accessed August 12, 2015. (http://www.nytimes. com/2015/04/27/business/dealbook/burdened-with-debt-law-school-graduates-struggle-in-job-market.html)

O'Shaughnessy, Lynn. "10 Reasons to Attend Canadian Universities," CBS News, October 20, 2010. Accessed August 4, 2015. (http://www.cbsnews.com/news/ 10-reasons-to-attend-canadian-universities)

Parchment.com. Accessed August 4, 2015. (http://www.parchment.com)

PayScale. "2014–2015 College Salary Report." Accessed August 4, 2015. (http://www. payscale.com/college-salary-report)

Peréz-Peña, Richard. "Dartmouth Cites Student Misconduct on Its Ban on Hard Liquor," *New York Times*, January 29, 2015. Accessed August 6, 2015. (http://www. nytimes.com/2015/01/30/us/in-response-to-student-misconduct-dartmouth-to-ban-hard-liquor-at-parties.html)

Phelan, James. *Beyond the Tenure Track: Fifteen Months in the Life of an English Professor.* Columbus, Ohio: Ohio State University Press, 1991.

Pierre, Kathy. "How Much Do You Study? Apparently 17 Hours a Week Is the Norm," *USA Today,* August 18, 2014. Accessed August 6, 2015. (http://college. usatoday.com/2014/08/18/how-much-do-you-study-apparently-17-hours-a-week-is-the-norm/)

"PLUS Loans." Federal Student Aid. Accessed August 3, 2015. (https://studentaid.ed. gov/types/loans/plus)

"Report of the Special Trustee Committee on Campus Unrest at Cornell," Office of University Publications, Cornell University, *Eric*, September 5, 1969. Accessed August 12, 2015. (http://eric.ed.gov/?id=ED036278)

Rosovksy, Henry. *The University: An Owner's Manual.* New York: Norton, 2000.

RT. "Top 10 Powerful Quotes from Putin's Historic Crimea Address," March 19, 2014. Accessed August 12, 2015. (http://rt.com/news/putin-address-ten-quotes-778/)

Ruiz, Rebecca R. "Applying to College in the United Kingdom," *New York Times*, September 22, 2011. Accessed August 4, 2015. (http://thechoice.blogs.nytimes. com/2011/09/22/applying-to-college-in-the-united-kingdom/)

Schonfeld, Zach. "Inside the Colleges That Killed Frats for Good," *Newsweek*, March 10, 2014. Accessed August 6, 2015. (http://www.newsweek.com/inside-colleges-killed-frats-good-231346)

Schumpeter [Adrian Wooldrige]. "Philosopher-Kings: Business Leaders Would Benefit from Studying Great Writers," *Economist*, October 4, 2014. Accessed August 11, 2015. (http://www.economist.com/news/business/21621778-business-leaders-would-benefit-studying-great-writers-philosopher-kings)

Schwarz, Daniel R. *In Defense of Reading: Teaching Literature in the Twenty-First Century.* Malden, Mass. and Oxford, UK: Wiley-Blackwell, 2006.

Skorton, David. "Op-Ed: A Call for Balanced Change in American Higher Education," *US News*, September 22, 2014. Accessed August 3, 2015. (http://www.usnews.com/ news/college-of-tomorrow/articles/2014/09/22/op-ed-a-call-for-balanced-change-in-american-higher-education)

Skorton, David. "A Pledge to End Fraternity Hazing," *New York Times*, August 23, 2011. Accessed August 6, 2015. (http://www.nytimes.com/2011/08/24/opinion/a-pledge-to-end-fraternity-hazing.html)

Spurgeon, Charles H. "The Treasury of David: Psalm 139," Spurgeon Archive. Accessed August 5, 2015. (http://www.spurgeon.org/treasury/ps139.htm)

Stevens, Wallace. "The Idea of Order at Key West," Poetry Foundation. Accessed August 13, 2015. (http://www.poetryfoundation.org/poem/172206)

Strogatz, Steven. *The Joy of X*. New York: Eamon Dolan/Houghton Mifflin Harcourt, 2012.

Strunk, William B., Jr. and E.B. White. *The Elements of Style*. New York: Longman, 1999.

Student Doctor Network. Accessed August 6, 2015. (http://www.studentdoctor.net)

Sutherland, Paige. "Amherst Cracks Down on Fraternities, Sororities," *Huffington Post*, August 6, 2014. (http://www.huffingtonpost.com/huff-wires/20140507/us-amherst-college-fraternities/)

Tolstoy, Leo. *Anna Karenina*, trans Richard Pevear and Larissa Volokhonsky. New York and London. Penguin, 2000–1.

Tolstoy, Leo. *Christianity and Patriotism* (1896). Accessed August 12, 2015. (http://en.wikiquote.org/wiki/Leo_Tolstoy)

Tolstoy, Leo. *War and Peace*, trans Richard Pevear and Larissa Volokhonsky. New York: Alfred A. Knopf, 2007.

Unz, Ron. "End Tuition at Elite Colleges to Attract More Applicants," *New York Times*, March 31, 2015. Accessed August 4, 2015. (http://www.nytimes.com/roomfordebate/2015/03/31/how-to-improve-the-college-admissions-process/end-tuition-at-elite-colleges-to-attract-more-applicants)

Wade, Nicholas. "Scientists Seek Ban on Method of Editing the Human Genome," *New York Times*, March 19, 2015. Accessed August 12, 2015. (http://www.nytimes.com/2015/04/16/opinion/nicholas-kristof-starving-for-wisdom.html?ref=opinion)

Warner, Joel and Clauset, Aaron. "The Academy's Dirty Secret: An Astonishingly Small Number of Elite Universities Produce an Overwhelming Number of America's Professors," *Slate*, February 23, 2015. Accessed August 12, 2015. (http://www.slate.com/articles/life/education/2015/02/university_hiring_if_you_didn_t_get_your_ph_d_at_an_elite_university_good.html)

Wood, Janice. "College Students in Study Spend 8 to 10 Hours Daily on Cell Phone," Psych Central. Accessed August 11, 2015. (http://www.slate.com/articles/life/education/2015/02/university_hiring_if_you_didn_t_get_you_ph_d_at_an_elite_university_good.html)

Zakaria, Fareed. *In Defense of a Liberal Education*. New York: W.W. Norton, 2015.

Zen College Life. "15 Frightening Facts about Sororities and Fraternities." Accessed August 6, 2015. (http://www.zencollegelife.com/15-frightening-facts-about-sororities-and-fraternities/)

Index

How to Succeed in College and Beyond: The Art of Learning, First Edition. Daniel R. Schwarz.
© 2016 John Wiley & Sons, Ltd. Published 2016 by John Wiley & Sons, Ltd.